$24.35
09-02

Southeast

LIFEWAYS

The Cherokee

RAYMOND BIAL

***B*ENCHMARK *B*OOKS**

MARSHALL CAVENDISH
NEW YORK

SERIES CONSULTANT: JOHN BIERHORST

ACKNOWLEDGMENTS

This book would not have been possible without the generous help of a number of individuals and organizations that have dedicated themselves to preserving the culture of the Cherokee Nation. I would like especially to thank Aaron Bradley, Clarence Wike, and all the good people at Oconoluftee Indian Village for their gracious hospitality while I was making photographs for *The Cherokee*. I am indebted to Joan Greene and the Museum of the Cherokee Indian for sharing key resources with me. I would also like to thank Tom Mooney and Charles Banks Wilson for their gracious help. I would also like to acknowledge the assistance of the Gilcrease Museum, the Philbrook Museum of Art, and the Cherokee National Historical Society for providing a number of wonderful photographs for this book.

I would like to express my deepest appreciation to my editor Kate Nunn for her enthusiasm and encouragement of this series and to consultant John Bierhorst for carefully reviewing the work-in-progress. As always, I would like to thank my wife, Linda, and my children Anna, Sarah, and Luke for their shining presence in my life.

Benchmark Books
Marshall Cavendish Corporation
99 White Plains Road Tarrytown, New York 10591-9001
Text copyright © 1999 by Raymond Bial Maps copyright
© 1999 by Marshall Cavendish Corporation
Illustration copyright © 1999 by Marshall Cavendish Corporation
Maps and illustration by Rodica Prato.
Library of Congress Cataloging-in-Publication Data
Bial, Raymond. The Cherokee / Raymond Bial.
p. cm. — (Lifeways) Includes bibliographical references and index.
Summary: Discusses the history, culture, social structure, beliefs, and customs of the Cherokee people.
ISBN 0-7614-0801-0 (lib. bdg.) 1. Cherokee Indians—Dwellings—Juvenile literature. 2. Cherokee Indians—History—Juvenile literature. 3. Cherokee Indians—Social life and customs—Juvenile literature.
[1. Cherokee Indians. 2. Indians of North America.] I. Title. II. Series: Bial, Raymond. Lifeways. E99.C5B48
1999 973'.049755—DC21 97-26574 CIP AC Rev.
Printed in Italy
5 6 4

Cover photos: Raymond Bial

The photographs in this book are used by permission and through the courtesy of: The Philbrook Museum of Art, Tulsa, Oklahoma: 1, 86-87; Raymond Bial: 6, 8-9, 11, 14, 16-17, 20-21, 22, 23, 24, 25, 26, 29, 34-35, 40-41, 46-47, 48, 50, 51, 54, 55, 56-57, 64-65, 67, 74, 82, 88-89, 92, 95, 96-97, 98-99, 100-101; Cherokee Heritage Center: 13, 27, 28, 43, 53, 58, 66; Gilcrease Museum, 32, 72, 112; Museum of the Cherokee Indian: 37, 52; Woolaroc Museum: 70-71; Earl Palmer/Appalachian Photograph Collection, Special Collections Department, University Libraries, Virginia Tech: 75; Charles Banks Wilson: 80; Western History Collection, University of Oklahoma Libraries, 102, 110, 115; Archive Photos: Hirz, 104, 109 (bottom); Corbis-Bettmann, 106; Yale University/Michael Marsland, 107; Library of Congress, 108, 109 (top).

This book is respectfully dedicated
to all the people
who have dedicated themselves
to keeping alive the traditional lifeways
of the Cherokee and helping others
understand the spirit
of the "real people."

Contents

Author's Note

At the dawn of the twentieth century, Native Americans were thought to be a vanishing race. However, despite four hundred years of warfare, deprivation, and disease, American Indians have not gone away. Countless thousands have lost their lives, but over the course of this century the populations of native tribes have grown tremendously. Even as American Indians struggle to adapt to modern Western life, they have also kept the flame of their traditions alive—the language, religion, stories, and the everyday ways of life. An exhilarating renaissance in Native American culture is now sweeping the nation from coast to coast.

The Lifeways books depict the social and cultural life of the major nations, from the early history of native peoples in North America to their present-day struggles for survival and dignity. Historical and contemporary photographs of traditional subjects, as well as period illustrations, are blended throughout each book so that readers may gain a sense of family life in a tipi, a hogan, or a longhouse.

No single book can comprehensively portray the intricate and varied lifeways of an entire tribe, or nation. I only hope that young people will come away with a deeper appreciation for the rich tapestry of Indian culture—both then and now—and a keen desire to learn more about these first Americans.

1. Origins

To the Cherokee, the mountains were home—from the shadows of the deepest valleys to the tops of the highest peaks.

"How the Earth Was Made"

IN THE BEGINNING ALL CREATURES DWELLED HIGH IN THE SKY. But after a time the sky became too crowded with people and animals. Finally, the little water beetle, or Beaver's Grandchild, flew down to explore the wide ocean below the sky. The water beetle skittered this way and that over the surface of the water, but could find no land. So he dived to the bottom of the ocean and brought up a tiny bit of mud, which grew and grew until it became an island.

All the people and animals were eager to come to Earth, but the ground was still very soft and wet. Birds flew down to see how fast it was drying, but there was no firm place on which to land and they became tired. Then the buzzard—who was no ordinary buzzard, but the grandfather of all buzzards—glided down to Earth. He flew very low and his wings struck the ground, making valleys. When his wings swept upward again he formed the Great Smoky Mountains. Worried that the entire world would become mountains and valleys, the creatures called the buzzard back to the sky, but the heart of Cherokee country remains full of mountains to this day.

When the land had dried, the people and animals came down from the sky, but the earth was dark. The Cherokee placed the sun in a track that arched over their island, but the sun was too close and hot. The red crayfish tried to shove the sun higher in the sky, but his shell was scorched. Then the shamans, or priests, pushed the sun up one handbreadth, but it was still too hot. They moved

The Cherokee lived beneath a canopy of trees that provided shade in summer and shelter from the winter wind.

it higher and higher until it was in just the right place under the arch of the sky—seven handbreadths high—which is why the shamans call the highest point in the sky "seventh height."

About two thousand years ago, the Cherokee made their way into the blue mist of the Great Smoky Mountains. Like all Native Americans, the Cherokee came to North America from the frozen stretches of Siberia. Most likely, they first migrated to what is now Texas or northern Mexico and then northward to the woods around the Great Lakes. There they warred with the Iroquois and were driven to the mountains of southern Appalachia. Following a woodland way of life, the Cherokee farmed and hunted. They lived in harmony with nature, gathering crab apples, grapes, cherries, hickory nuts, walnuts, and chestnuts in the woods and meadows around them. The Cherokee spoke an Iroquoian language and were distant ancestral relations of the Iroquois of New York and Canada. In their own language, the Cherokee call themselves *Aniyvwiya* (pronounced a-ni-yoo-wi-ya), which means "real people" or "principal people." They probably got the name *Cherokee* from the neighboring Creek, whose word *tciloki* (pronounced chi-lo-ki) means "people of a different speech."

By the late 1700s, there were about twelve thousand men, women, and children in the Cherokee Nation, which was considered one of the "civilized" tribes by settlers because the people had adopted European ways. Located in eastern Tennessee, the western Carolinas, northern Georgia, and northeastern Alabama, the Cherokee homeland was one of the last Indian strongholds east of the Mississippi River. Their land included the Appalachians of the Upland South, with all the waters flowing down either side of the Great Smoky Mountains. White traders described them as honest, yet fierce in battle. To be clean in body

For hundreds of years, the Cherokee people made their homes in small villages, where they lived in harmony with nature and each other.

The Cherokee have always respected the healing power of water. Living near sparkling clear rivers, they often bathed to cleanse both body and soul.

and spirit, they "went to water," bathing often in clear pools and mountain streams. They considered water, the sun, and fire to be holy gifts of *Kanati*, the Great Spirit.

The People and the Land

Like other American Indians, the Cherokee lived within the natural world. They blended with the mountains, streams, and trees, like the deer, black bears, and other animals that made their home in the forests and grassy valleys called coves.

The Blue Ridge and Great Smoky Mountains, where the Cherokee lived, extend into present-day Tennessee and North Carolina. The ranges were named for the cool, blue haze that floats over their peaks. Pine trees jut into the sky on those high peaks, and hardwoods—oak, hickory, sweet gum, blue ash, and dogwood—blanket the slopes. The Cherokee regarded the red cedar, a fragrant wood that resists decay in damp climates, as the most sacred of trees. The mountains are also interlaced with streams, and clear water tumbles over boulders as it races down the slopes. As the Cherokee hunted and foraged in these mountains, they always stepped lightly, paying homage to the plants and animals that sustained them.

The stories, beliefs, and rituals of the Cherokee are woven into the fabric of the land. It is a beloved place, which they have called home for hundreds of years.

2. Villages

Sturdy log walls with points jutting skyward protected Cherokee villages from attacks by their enemies as well as by wild animals.

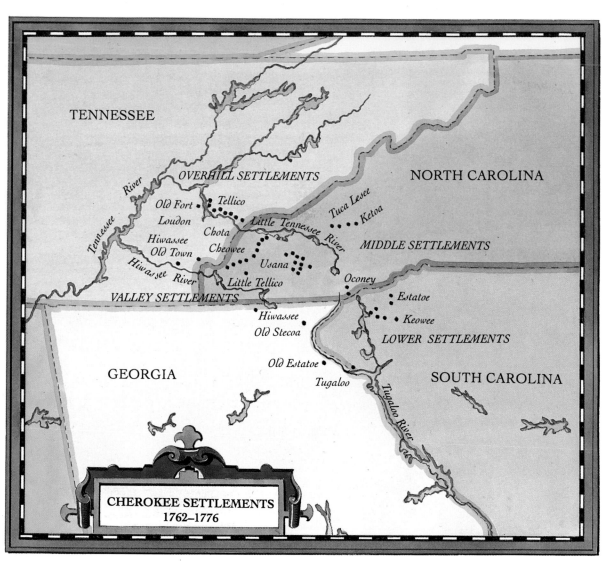

TENNESSEE

River

Tennessee

NORTH CAROLINA

OVERHILL SETTLEMENTS

Old Fort • • *Tellico*

Tuca Lesee • • *Ketoa*

Loudon

Little Tennessee River

Chota

Hiwassee • *Cheowee*

MIDDLE SETTLEMENTS

Old Town

Usana

Hiwassee River

Little Tellico

Oconey

VALLEY SETTLEMENTS

• *Estatoe*

• *Hiwassee*

• *Keowee*

Old Stecoa

LOWER SETTLEMENTS

• *Old Estatoe*

GEORGIA

Tugaloo

SOUTH CAROLINA

Tugaloo River

CHEROKEE SETTLEMENTS
1762–1776

*C*herokee villages were clustered along the banks of an intricate network of
rivers in four different areas of the Great Smoky Mountains.

THE CHEROKEE LIVED IN SMALL VILLAGES. IN 1730 THERE WERE OVER forty villages generally clustered into four groups in the Appalachian Mountains: Valley Settlements, Overhill Settlements, Middle Settlements, and the Lower Settlements. The heart of the Cherokee Nation was in the Middle Settlements on the south bank of the Little Tennessee River in the western Carolinas. Four to six hundred people lived in each of the villages strung along valley streams and rivers. Communities were linked by seven networks of trails over which the Cherokee traveled to trade goods with the Iroquois, Chickasaw, Catawba, and other tribes as far away as the Gulf of Mexico.

Houses

Protected by a high log wall called a palisade, each town centered on the council house, a large, round, post-and-beam building with a domed roof. It was designed with seven sides so that each of the clans in the town—Wolf, Deer, Bird, Paint, Blue, Wind, and Wild Potato—could be equally close to the center. Men gathered daily in the council house, which varied in size according to the population of the town, to smoke tobacco and discuss village matters.

In each of the Cherokee towns there were seven clans, which included extended family members—not just parents, brothers, and sisters, but also aunts, uncles, cousins, and grandparents. Each clan was responsible for feeding, clothing, and sheltering its own. One did not marry into one's own clan; when a couple

embers of the seven clans gathered in the council house. Because the council house had seven sides, each clan was seated an equal distance from the center.

married, the husband typically came to live with his wife's family or in a separate home within her clan. The sections of each clan were marked off by dirt ridges, lines of stones, or rows of sticks.

Originally, the Cherokee lived in homes similar to pit houses.

Dug into hillsides, these homes had log walls and a doorway on
the slope. The roof of the primitive homes was made of bark,
thatch, or earth. Inside, there was a raised hearth on the dirt floor,
but no chimney—smoke rose through the open doorway. The
walls of this cavelike dwelling were probably covered with bark or

woven mats. Homes were grouped together in villages that probably also had sweat lodges, storehouses, and small buildings.

Later, the Cherokee began to construct sturdy, permanent homes with clay walls and thatched roofs. To make these homes, they set large posts into the ground about three feet apart, with smaller poles placed between them. They then wove supple branches or split canes between the posts to make walls, which they plastered with a thick coat of clay mixed with grass. Sometimes the Cherokee whitewashed their homes with lime obtained by crushing burnt clam shells. They made the domed roofs in the same manner as the walls, then covered the woven canes with bark or thatch to shed the rain. These houses had no windows and only a small doorway covered by an animal skin or

Early Cherokee homes had thick clay-covered walls and thatched roofs. There was a smoke hole in the top and a single doorway, but no windows.

mat to keep out the cold. Inside, a basin was scooped out in the middle of the floor for the fire, and a circular hearthstone for baking bread was placed next to it. Women kept a fire burning continually, with threads of whitish gray smoke rising through a small hole in the roof.

Cherokee houses gradually evolved into square or rectangular homes with gabled roofs. These buildings were similar in structure to contemporary homes, except that they had a post-and-beam frame, thick clay walls, and saplings lashed down on the roof to hold the shingles in place. They had one or two stories and several rooms to accommodate large families, many of whom slept in bunk beds. During the warm summer months, it is believed that the Cherokee lived in large homes with woven reed walls and a

From settlers who moved into the region, the Cherokee learned to build log cabins with shingled roofs and red clay chinking between the logs.

long porch across the front. After the Cherokee came into contact with English settlers in the mid-1700s, they began to build and live in log cabins.

Furnishings

The Cherokee kept little furniture and only a few possessions in their homes: rugs, baskets, clay pots, stools, and beds, along with clothing and a little food. They made spoons from buffalo horns and fashioned many articles from wood and gourds, including masks to frighten enemies. They used tobacco widely, especially in ceremonies, and they carved pipe bowls from soapstone, then fitted them with wooden stems. Placed at one end of the home, their beds had short posts for legs, with white oak or ash splints woven on a sapling frame. People slept on rush or split-

Cherokee people placed mats or bearskins on wood frame beds, which lined the inside walls of their homes.

*T*he Cherokee made their own tools and household utensils, such as these gourds, which they turned into dippers and ladles.

cane mats on the beds, covered with skins from bears, elk, deer, or mountain lions.

Women made striking rugs from hemp threads which they painted with imaginative and colorful designs. They also wove baskets that were both lovely and useful for storage. Early Cherokee baskets were made from hemp fibers or the inner bark of mulberry trees. Later, strips of river cane and white oak were used to weave sturdy and beautiful baskets, often with a bold zig-zag double weave called a lightning design. The Cherokee stored food in these baskets as well as in pots, jugs, and jars. They kept some food in the home for daily use, but placed most corn, beans,

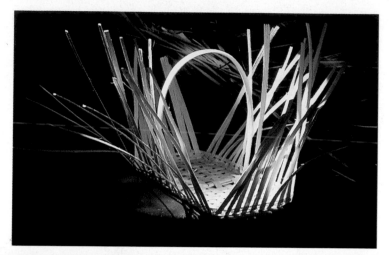

 *C*herokee women have always been highly skilled with their hands; they are renowned for the quality of their white oak and river cane baskets. Here a white oak basket is just being started (above). Women artfully weave a design into the finished basket (below).

and other provisions in village storehouses made of white oak, hickory, poplar, and sassafras. Raised four to five feet off the ground, these buildings protected the corn harvest from rodents and rain.

Cherokee women shaped pottery entirely by hand. Using a mixture of light, sandy clay and fine, dark clay dug from riverbanks, they formed coils, which they then pinched and smoothed with their fingers to make a jar or pot. Or they simply used their fingers to form a cup or bowl. Sometimes they used stones and shell scrapers to smooth the clay surface, then stamped a design

Cherokee children learned by watching their parents. Here a mother teaches her son how to make pottery. Note the carved mask in the foreground.

*F*ire provided heat and a means of cooking food as well as hardening clay pottery.

on the vessel with a carved wooden paddle. The Cherokee dried their pottery for three days, then fired the pieces on a hearth of flat stones. They placed the pottery with the open mouths toward the fire for about one hour, until the clay turned slightly brown. They then rolled the pots and jars directly into the embers, mouth down, and covered them with dried bark, which burned away in an hour. Finally, they threw a handful of bran or broken-up corn cobs into the vessel, which quickly ignited. The pottery was then turned upside down to smoke and waterproof the inside.

During the coldest part of the winter families stayed in a hothouse, a stout log frame built into a slope and covered with a mound of earth. A fire was kept burning throughout the day to warm the house, then banked at night. Since there was no smoke hole and only a small doorway, the hothouse would become too smoky if the fire was left burning at night. People slept on wide benches lining the walls, and the dwellings were so warm that bedcovers and clothes was hardly necessary.

Shamans often used their hothouses as sweat lodges for ceremonies and medical treatments. They heated river rocks in the fire and raked them out over the ground. Then they poured a liquid of steeped wild parsnip roots or bark from persimmon, mulberry, cherry, or poplar trees over the hot stones. After their sweat baths, men took a cold plunge in the river. Around the flickering orange fire of the winter homes, mythkeepers recalled the sacred legends of the Cherokee past.

Government

Each town was represented by a council. The council was headed by a shaman, who had no authority but advised on spiritual and medical matters. There were two chiefs—the White chief (also known as the most beloved man), who handled daily concerns of the town, and the Red chief, who offered advice regarding war parties, victory dances, and the spirited games that were a vital part of the Cherokee way of life. Seven elder men were chosen from each clan. These men usually led discussions, although all Cherokee men participated. The council discussed town concerns, including religious matters, and decided by consensus, meaning general agreement. Cherokee society had little need of formal laws. Seeking harmony in relations with each other, they maintained order by social pressure and negotiation among disputing individuals or clans.

The Cherokee were a highly organized people, not only within each village, but in the nation as a whole, with two forms of government—the White for civil or peacetime affairs and the Red

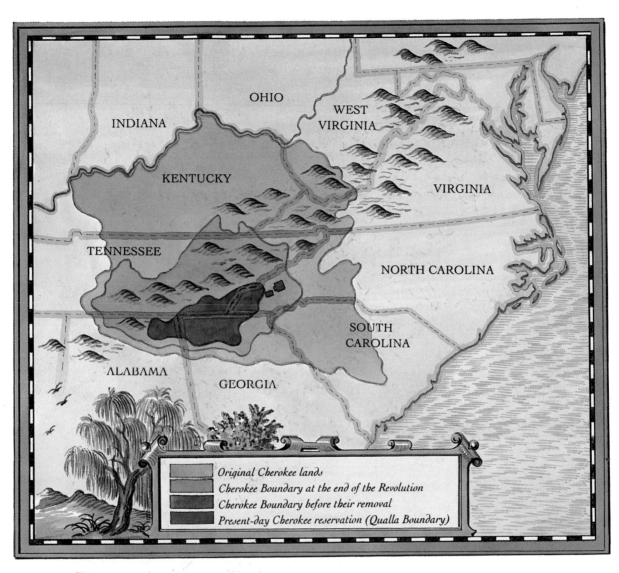

Legend:
- Original Cherokee lands
- Cherokee Boundary at the end of the Revolution
- Cherokee Boundary before their removal
- Present-day Cherokee reservation (Qualla Boundary)

This map shows the gradual loss of the Cherokee homeland from the American Revolution to the present day.

32 *The quiet pride and dignity of the Cherokee people are revealed in the face of Cunne Shote, a Cherokee chief, as painted by Francis Parsons.*

for waging war. The White chief was the religious head or high priest as well. Next in importance to the chief was the right-hand man, or *itausta*, and then the chief speaker. The chief had seven councilors, including the right-hand man, who formed the main government. The Red organization consisted of a group of officials corresponding in rank to the White leaders, except that they were responsible only for military activities. The White organization had slightly more power because the Red chief was selected by the White chief.

There were other important people within Cherokee government, notably the beloved woman, an elderly matron who was honored for her wisdom and goodness. Seven women, usually the eldest women in the nation, also took part in many council ceremonies.

The national government met in a large seven-sided building situated on a high mound in the capital. The capital was not fixed at first, but was always in the village of the White chief, although Echota eventually became the traditional capital. As in the town council house, the seating arrangement was highly formalized, with the White chief occupying the seat of honor. Here, Cherokee leaders held elaborate national ceremonies, assembled war parties, and administered laws.

3. Lifeways

Women stood at the center of Cherokee society. They raised the children and managed the homes, because the men were often away from the village.

MEN WERE OFTEN AWAY—HUNTING, FIGHTING, AND TRADING with outsiders—while women raised crops in fields and gardens and looked after the children. Since they remained at home, the women headed households and owned most property. Although men led discussions in the council house, women had a central role and a great deal of power in the Cherokee community. A woman and man from different clans could freely choose to marry each other, and husbands and wives decided together where they wanted to live. Yet the house belonged to the wife, as did the children, who were raised by her and taught by her brothers. Since the man married into the woman's clan, he was considered an outsider, but his children became part of the clan. Cherokee families were matrilineal, meaning children traced their names and family history through their mothers. Even if children had a white father, they were full members of the nation and the clan, as long as their mother was Cherokee.

Cycle of Life

Birth. When a Cherokee woman learned that she was going to have a baby she told her husband, who spread the good news throughout the village. He then built a special dwelling where she confined herself for the last three months of her pregnancy. She had to submit to many rules and rituals, the most notable of which was that at each new moon she was taken to water. Accompanied by her husband, mother, and a shaman, she prayed to be purified. The shaman poured water on the crown of her head and chest, then he attempted to foresee the child's future.

Children were loved and cherished in Cherokee homes and, whether a boy or a girl, the birth of a baby was cause for great joy throughout the village.

When the woman went into labor she might be assisted by as many as four women. However, the expectant mother usually had little difficulty in childbirth, and her mother or grandmother provided all necessary help. Sometimes a shaman might be present to pray for a quick and safe delivery, but otherwise men were not allowed in the dwelling.

During childbirth the mother-to-be knelt on a robe with her legs spread. If the newborn fell on its back, it was good, but if the baby landed on its chest, it was considered a bad sign. The newborn was then immediately wrapped in a cloth, taken to a stream, and immersed until the cloth floated away to remove any ill fortune.

When the baby was one or two days old, the shaman waved it four times over a fire and offered a blessing. When the baby was either four or seven days old, the shaman took it to a stream and prayed to the Creator that it might have a long and happy life.

Then a naming ceremony took place in which a respected elderly woman christened the baby. Often, she selected a name based on the baby's resemblance to an object, something that had happened at the birth, or a unique trait of the child. Later, the child might be renamed because of a heroic deed, such as killing a bear. Names gave special identity to the child, and could never be misused. If a shaman's cures failed during treatment of an illness, he concluded that the patient's name was no longer effective. He then took the patient to water and gave him or her a new name.

Childhood. For the first two years the child was bathed daily in the river. At age four or five, the father or a mother's brother took charge of the boys, who were taught hunting, fighting, and other ways of the men. A few boys, who came to be called "devoted sons," were encouraged to become shamans when they grew up.

Girls learned the roles of women by helping their mothers and older sisters in the home and fields.

Mothers and fathers loved and indulged their children, for which they were criticized by settlers. Yet children honored and respected their parents, as well as the elderly people of the village.

A young woman having her first menstrual period went to a separate camp, away from her family. No one was allowed to touch her. She could not even handle her own food, and another woman had to feed her. After seven days, to purify herself, she bathed and washed her clothing as well as anything else she had touched. She then returned to her clan, and if she wished, she could marry a young man in the village.

Marriage. There were strict laws against marrying anyone from one's own clan. At one time the penalty for this offense was death; later whipping became the punishment. Typically, when a young man wished to marry a young woman from another clan, he spoke with his parents, then asked the consent of her parents. He might also speak with a brother from each of the clans. If everyone agreed, a date was set, and the shaman was informed of the marriage plans.

On the morning of the wedding the shaman laid two roots in the palm of his hand. Facing east, he prayed for the couple. If the roots did not move or if one root withered, the couple would not live well together. If the roots moved together, it was a good sign and the marriage took place.

When a person died, as part of the funeral ceremony, members of the family bathed in a nearby stream to purify themselves in the rushing water.

Death. When a person, especially an elderly father, was about to die, he gathered his children around him. He offered advice about their futures and reminded them of Cherokee customs. Young children were then sent away, because only the shaman and adult relatives were allowed to be present at the deathbed.

Women wept profusely, and at the moment of death, they cried out, repeating the name of the deceased over and over. During the seven days of mourning, men seldom cried, but

they smeared ashes on their heads and put on worn clothing.

A relative closed the eyelids and washed the body. Soon after the death a shaman who was responsible for burials arrived at the home. He buried the loved one in the dirt floor beneath the place of death, under the hearth, or just outside the dwelling. A distinguished chief was buried under his seat in the council house. Belongings were either buried with the deceased or burned at the gravesite.

Everyone in the household was now considered unclean, and furnishings, clothing, and food had to be thrown away. The shaman then ritually purified the house. He thoroughly cleaned the hearth and kindled a new fire. Over this fire he brewed a pot of tea made from a special weed. The family members drank this tea and washed themselves with it. To cleanse the house further, the shaman smoked a pipe and built a fire with cedar boughs and another special weed. He then hid what was left of the purifying ritual in a hollow tree.

Lastly, he took the family members to a stream and prayed over them as they strode into the water. They allowed their garments to be carried away with the current and when they came out of the water they put on new clothing.

When the mourners returned to their purified home, the shaman gave them a string of beads to ease their grief and a piece of tobacco to "enlighten their eyes," so they could bravely look to the future.

Food and Clothing

Against a backdrop of hazy blue mountains, Cherokee women farmed the rich soil of coves, or valleys. Their primary crops were corn, beans, pumpkins, squash, sunflowers, and tobacco. Cherokee mothers and daughters grew three different kinds of corn for roasting, boiling, and grinding into meal for bread. Fields and gardens were owned by the entire clan. Each woman helped to raise and harvest the precious yellow grain, which was stored in a common building. No one hoarded food; everyone took only

In addition to heading the household Cherokee women were also responsible for many laborious tasks, such as grinding the corn that was used in a variety of dishes throughout the year.

as much corn as they needed to feed their family. The Cherokee were a generous people who believed in equality and sharing among themselves. Each year they held ceremonies in which they destroyed possessions to show how little their property mattered to them.

Cherokee women prepared all the meals and taught their daughters how to cook and manage their home life. They fried, roasted, or boiled various dishes that were so delicious they are still eaten today. The Cherokee ate fish and meat, primarily deer, rabbit, squirrel, and turkey, along with beans, squash, and corn. A typical meal might include warm boiled beans with bread made from a bean and corn batter that was wrapped in cornhusks and baked over hot coals. Corn, often in the form of parched cornmeal, was the most important food; it was prepared in different ways and included in many dishes. To parch corn, women cooked a mixture of cornmeal and wood ashes in a pot over an open fire. Parched corn kept well on long hunting trips and was used in a variety of foods, such as swamp potatoes, stewed groundhog, and wild grape soup.

The Cherokee made some very interesting dishes: yellow jacket soup, chestnut bread, hickory nut soup, "slick-go-downs" (mushrooms), cornbread baked on bark, "leather breeches" (green beans), "knee-deeps" (small frogs); and they drank spicewood tea, "possum grape drink," and "parched corn drink." The following recipe traditionally took several hours to prepare over an open fire. With the modern version, you can substitute ingredients and make a similar dish in much less time.

Corn and Beans

Ingredients:

Indian corn (large white); may substitute
  16-ounce can of hominy corn
Colored beans; may substitute 16-ounce can
  of kidney beans
Molasses to taste

The Cherokee usually removed the "skin" of the kernels with lye to make hominy, then cooked it together with colored beans in an iron pot. Sometimes they added pumpkin or a mixture of cornmeal, beaten walnuts and hickory nuts, and sometimes they added molasses as a sweetener. They either ate this dish fresh or after it began to sour.

In your recipe, drain hominy corn and kidney beans. Place in a cooking pot and add enough water to cover the mixture. Simmer for 10 minutes. Sweeten with a little molasses or maple syrup.

*C*orn, the most important food of the Cherokee, was ground by hand with a mortar and pestle.

Cherokee women either grew or gathered what they needed to feed their families. In addition to basic foods, maple syrup was boiled down in the spring to make crumbly sugar; powdered honey locust pods were also used as a sweetener.

Myths, magic, and legends permeated Cherokee life, even in the preparation of meals. To hurry the cooking of food, women sometimes recited the following charm about the red crayfish, a small creature that cooks rapidly: "Now! *Ha!* Now very quickly I have just come to put the Red Crayfish in the pot!"

To make clothing, women tanned the hides of deer, beaver, mountain lion, otter, and other animals, although they mostly used buckskin from tanned deerskins. With fishbone needles,

To this day, the Cherokee practice many traditional crafts, including the weaving of sashes in bold patterns. Traditionally, the colorful sashes were worn as headbands or belts.

they sewed wraparound skirts for their daughters and themselves. During cold weather they also wore capes of buffalo calfskin with the hair turned inside. Later, they adorned cloth skirts with rows of brass beads or leather belts fastened with buckles. Men and boys wore breechcloths made from a piece of buckskin drawn up between their legs and around their waist. In summer they also sometimes wore buckskin shirts but most often went barechested. In winter their shirts were made from the skin of bear, beaver, otter, and panther, with the fur inside for greater warmth. Around the villages, everyone either went barefoot or, during cold weather, wore soft deerskin moccasins. When hunting, men wore tall deerskin boots fringed with fawns' hooves or turkey feet.

The Cherokee often decorated their clothing. Women spun possum fur into threads which they dyed red, yellow, or dark brown. To make black threads they spun bear fur. These colored threads were woven into the caps, belts, and garters with which the Cherokee adorned themselves. Men sometimes wore capes or mantles made from buckskin or turkey and eagle feathers. Prominent warriors wore bands of otter skin on their heads, upper arms, and just below their knees. The chiefs' robes were often quite elaborate—made of white or yellow leather adorned with crane feathers or strings of deer hooves, with sleeves of raccoon fur. Chiefs' headdresses were often made from a roll of raccoon skins dyed yellow or, for the peace chief, from white crane feathers.

Women skillfully decorate belts with bold designs made with beads of many brilliant colors.

Cherokee men taught boys how to make darts for their blowguns with sharp sticks. Each was tipped with thistle fluff.

Hunting and Warfare

When boys grew up, their days were filled with warfare, trading, ball games, and hunting and fishing. During the coldest half of the year, Cherokee warriors patrolled their land, engaging in bloody skirmishes to drive back the Creek, Chickasaw, Catawba, and other tribes that tried to encroach upon the mountains. The Cherokee also made raids on lands claimed by other tribes. Sometimes they sold captured enemies as slaves. If one of their warriors was slain, they sought vengeance. His spirit would not rest until the murderer himself was killed.

Cherokee men were active traders. They traded silver ornaments they had crafted, as well as deerskins and beaver pelts, with other tribes and European traders. A man could become wealthy, but if he did he had to deal with the disapproval of others

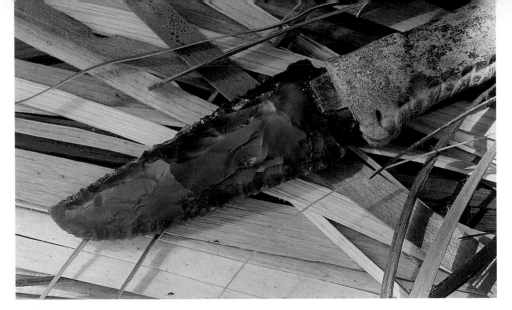

A long with arrowheads, the Cherokee made flint knives for scraping hides, cutting leather, splitting cane for baskets, and many other tasks.

in the clan and town who were not as well-off. They might scorn his wealth, and the shamans might wish him ill.

Like other eastern tribes, the Cherokee played a ball game similar to lacrosse. Called "the friend or companion of battle," or simply "little brother of war," these stickball games were very rough—there were often broken bones, torn muscles, cuts, and bruises. Elaborate rituals preceded the game. If someone wanted a contest, he gathered his friends and sent a challenge to another town. If the town accepted the challenge, people were selected for various tasks: an elderly man to oversee the game, a person to sing for the players, another to whoop, and a musician for seven women who danced on the seventh night of preparations for the game.

The night before the game, players danced together around the

In lacrosse, Cherokee men tested their strength, endurance, and ability to withstand pain. Before the games, they prepared their minds as well as their bodies.

fire with their ball sticks, pretending that they were playing. Then they hung up their sticks, went to a brisk stream, and bathed seven times, after which they went to bed. At daybreak, the shaman took them to the creek again. During their preparations the players were not allowed to go near women and they could not eat meat or anything hot or salty. Seven women were chosen to prepare meals of cold bread and a drink of parched cornmeal and water. The men could not be served by women, so boys brought the food to them. During the day the men were scratched with rattlesnake fangs or turkey quills to toughen them for the "little brother of war."

The two teams gathered on a large field where goalposts were

*T*raditionally, only men played lacrosse, yet this modern re-enactment accurately captures the spirit and action of the game.

set up at each end. Players paired off, the referee threw the ball up in the air between the two captains, and a mad scramble ensued. The game was "anything goes," and there was biting, gouging, choking, scratching, twisting arms and legs, and banging each other with the wooden rackets. The object of the game was to carry the ball between the goals twelve times. The first team with twelve wooden pegs stuck in the ground by the shaman won the game. There was no time limit and often the game went on until dark. There was also no time-out or substitution. If a player was injured, he and the opponent with whom he was paired both left the game. Cherokee gathered from throughout the mountains to watch and bet on these hotly contested games.

When they weren't trading, fighting, and playing ball games, men hunted for animals, which provided clothing as well as food for the village. Women cured, or tanned, deer hides into supple buckskin. The Cherokee stalked bear, deer, and elk with bows and arrows, and hunters wore deerskins complete with antlers to disguise themselves. They killed rabbits, squirrels, turkeys, and other small game with blowguns and darts. Skilled hunters blew the feathered darts through long hollowed-out canes with remarkable accuracy.

The Cherokee hunted rabbits, squirrels, and other small animals with a blowgun through which they shot a dart with a very sharp point.

Expert fishermen, the Cherokee used spears, bows and arrows, and hooks and lines to catch trout and catfish in the clear streams splashing down the mountainsides. Sometimes they fished from canoes made from hollowed-out logs. They also made clever wooden traps and baskets, which they dipped like nets into the water. Other times they dammed a stream and threw mashed chestnuts into the water to stun the fish. The Cherokee then easily collected by hand as many fish as they needed. When they broke up the dam, the rest of the fish recovered and swam away.

By burning and chopping large, straight logs, the Cherokee made dugouts, which they paddled down the clear mountain rivers.

4. Beliefs

Cherokee beliefs were rooted in the natural world
in which they made their home.

***B**oys were taught to blend into the land around them in order to learn the ways of the woods and the water. They learned to become good hunters and to understand their place in nature.*

BOYS WERE TAUGHT TO HUNT, FISH, AND FIGHT BY THE MEN in their clan, notably their mother's brothers, although sometimes all the young men in a town were instructed together. Boys were both praised and chided, but never struck, which was a sign of disrespect. They were allowed only two meals a day to instill a good appetite and willpower. A young hunter first had to learn the ways of the animals—to become one with them by entering their habitat. He was left by a stream to study the animals that came to drink at the edge, or he was sent high up a mountain, where he learned to hide in the green leaves and shadows. During his training as a hunter, he went all day without food to learn discipline. He was taught to be as silent as his own breath, from daybreak to dusk, neither speaking nor making a sound, so that he could better listen to the voices of the woods. Hunting was a way of life, and a boy learned not to change nature, but to find a place for himself within it. Later, if a young man wished to become a shaman, he could be apprenticed, but only after he had learned to be a good hunter and warrior.

The young hunter learned that because people had wastefully killed too much game in the past, the animals had cursed them with disease. Certain plants, known only to the shamans, provided cures. A young man believed that if he sprinkled tobacco on a heap of ashes at home and it caught fire, he would have a good hunt. If the tobacco did not ignite, he would find no game. A hunter knew not to kill the wolf, which was considered a messenger from the spirit world. One could sit by the fire at night,

The Little People

Most southeastern tribes, including the Cherokee, believed in the little people, who both charmed and pestered the men, women, and children of the villages.

listen to the wolves' distant, mournful howls, and learn much. If a hunter killed a wolf, game would vanish, and his bow would become useless until purified by the shaman. The hunter could also place the weapon in a swift river overnight or give it to a child to play with as a toy for a while. Yet he had to remember that the wolf always sought revenge—death for death. The young hunter could protect himself by reciting a prayer and bathing morning and evening in a stream.

The Little People

As they grew up, children were praised and entertained; they were given furry toys and allowed to have pets. They were also thrilled by stories about the imaginary little people who inhabited the land around them. Called *yunwi tsunsdi*, the little people were Cherokee—they spoke Cherokee and ate corn, beans, and game. Just one to three feet tall, the little men had long gray hair and beards and often wore hats of several colors. The little women, who looked and dressed like the Cherokee, were lovely and delicate. They danced at celebrations and sat long hours in the council house, telling stories and discussing important matters of the day.

Where were the little people? They were hiding in the bushes, parents told their children, or behind the misty veil of a waterfall. They were everywhere, possibly behind the nearest tree, but they could not be seen. Most often, they were heard in the songs of birds or the crash of thunder. The little people were often kind, helping young Cherokee when they were lost—they knew all the paths in the woods. They were good company for lonely people, and when a grandmother died they showed her the way to the Great Spirit. If children ever saw a little person, they were not to tell anyone for seven days, or bad luck would befall them. But the little people were not always helpful. When rocks tumbled down a hillside, one could be sure the little people were up there giggling at their mischief.

Legends

The religion of the Cherokee people was not based on the idea of a separate god. Instead, they felt a divine presence in everything around them—animals, plants, earth, wind, and sky. They saw themselves living in a world between the earth and sky. To them, all things in nature were equal to humans, and they respected the environment. The spirit of nature was also reflected in their legends. Many of these, such as "How the Milky Way Came To Be," "The First Fire," and "The Origin of Strawberries," dealt with the beginning of things in nature. Other stories, such as "Why the Mink Smells," "Why the Buzzard's Head Is Bare," and "The Rattlesnake's Vengeance," explained the ways of certain animals, sometimes in a humorous manner.

Here is a legend about the possum, which tells how its tail came to be bare. The story is also a lighthearted lesson about the consequence of being too vain.

"Why the Possum's Tail is Bare"

Long ago, Possum had a long, bushy tail. He was so proud of it that he brushed it every day and sang about it every night. He bragged about it so much that Rabbit, whose tail had been pulled off by Bear, became jealous and decided to play a trick on Possum.

There was to be a great council meeting and dance for all the animals. Possum agreed to come, but only if he was to be given a seat of honor. "I have such a handsome tail I should sit where everyone can see me," he explained. Rabbit agreed and even offered to send Cricket to comb his tail. In the morning Cricket went to Possum's house to get him ready for the dance. Possum stretched himself out and shut his eyes while Cricket combed his tail and wrapped a string around it to keep it smooth. But all the while Cricket was clipping off the hair to the roots.

That night Possum went to the dance and found the best seat ready for him, just as Rabbit had promised. When it was his turn to dance he loosened the red string and stepped onto the floor. "See my beautiful tail," he sang. Everyone shouted as he danced. "See what a pretty color it has," he bragged. "See how bushy it is!" The other animals shouted more loudly, and Possum was delighted. "See how my tail sweeps the ground." Then he noticed that the animals were laughing—and at him! He looked down at his tail and saw that there wasn't a hair left—it was as bare as a lizard's tail! He was so astonished that he couldn't say a word. He rolled helpless on the ground, feet in the air, and grinned just as the possum does to this day when taken by surprise.

Ceremonies and Dances

Over the course of the year the Cherokee held several great festivals either in the council house or at a sacred place called the square ground or dance ground. An opening in the forest canopy, the square ground was surrounded by rows of log seats under sloped roofs, with a bushy-topped tree rising from the very center.

Dances and celebrations were at the heart of Cherokee life. The square ground, where festivals were held, was a sacred place.

Ceremonies held there related to the seasons and the Cherokee's religious beliefs. Among these were the first new moon of spring, green corn (a time of thanksgiving and renewal in which people gave thanks to the corn spirit for an abundant harvest), October new moon, and renewal of brotherhood (also called reconciliation) ceremonies.

*P*eople solemnly ready themselves for a dance in their village.

As part of these seasonal events, the Cherokee held many lively dances in which water drums, gourd rattles, and turtle shell rattles were used as musical instruments. In the uka dance, the chief, or *uka*, himself offered thanksgiving in a spirit of rejoicing. Two persons were especially important in dances: the leader, who preserved order and made sure the dance was carried out properly, and the lead singer.

The green corn dance was originally part of the green corn ceremony, which celebrated the first harvest. This was one of the most important festivals of the Cherokee year. The warrior dance was performed before men went to war. There were also friendship dances, in which both men and women participated. Women danced either with their husbands or, if they were single, with their brothers or a young man from their clan. The round dance, or *atayohi*, was a special dance that concluded the all-night sessions of dancing. Led by a woman wearing leg rattles, the women danced counter-clockwise to four songs. As the songs became faster, the men paired off with the women. The Cherokee also danced whenever they wished to celebrate a good hunt or other joyful event.

The rhythm and beat of dances were carried by the drums (left). The tone of these drums could be varied by dampening the skin with water. Rattles were often fashioned from the shell of a box turtle (right).

During the eagle dance, the most important Cherokee ceremony, performers carried wands made from the feathers of the great bird.

The Cherokee believed that the eagle had magical powers, and the eagle dance (also called the victory dance) was very important to their way of life. The eagle dance was performed when one of the great birds was killed for its feathers, to welcome the spirit of the eagle to the village. Divided into three parts, the dance celebrated victory and honored the eagle for giving its feathers. Dancers either carried a feather wand and a rattle in each hand or a wand in both hands and danced to the beat of turtle shell rattles and water drums. Since the eagle and rattlesnake were believed to be deadly enemies, the dance was held only in the winter when the snake was asleep. If the rattlesnake heard the dancing and singing, it would become more deadly. Other accounts say the dance was not held in the summer because it would bring on an early frost.

Women joined in the eagle dance. They danced with feather wands, and a lead woman wore turtle shell rattles strapped to her knees. Participants formed two rings, the women in an inner circle, and they danced around a tree in the center of the square ground, waving the wands as they moved. There were different sets of songs and a variety of steps. It was critically important that the dancers not drop their wands or even allow them to touch the ground. It was believed that anyone who did so would soon die.

5·Changing World

"Whole nations have melted away like balls of snow before the sun." —Dragging Canoe

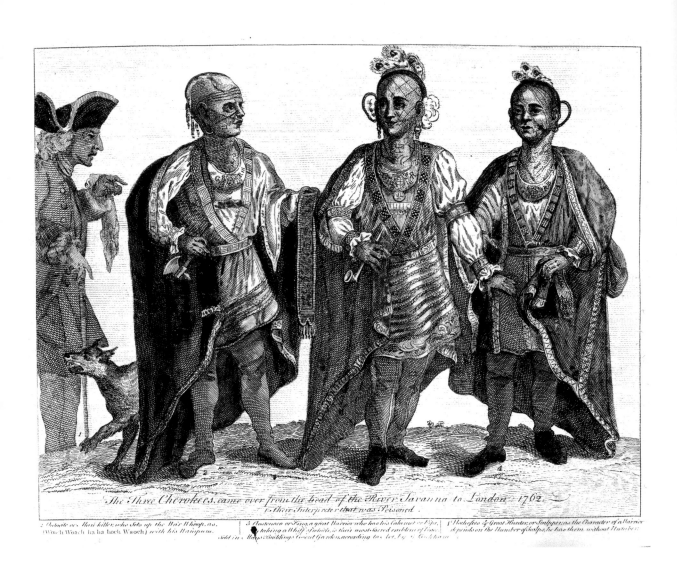

The Three Cherokees, came over from the head of the River Savanna to London 1762.
Their Interpreter that was Poisoned.

1n 1730, these young Cherokee were escorted by Sir Alexander Cumming to
England to meet King George II. One of them was Attakullakulla.

THIS IS HOW THE CHEROKEE LIVED AT THE TIME THEY CAME into contact with European explorers. Hernando de Soto first encountered the Cherokee during an expedition in 1540, and the Spanish explorer was impressed by their advanced society. Later, French traders made their way into Cherokee country, but after the first permanent settlement at Jamestown, Virginia, their most frequent contacts were with the English. By the end of the 1600s, European influences were beginning to change the Cherokee way of life. As trade increased, particularly in deerskins, men rose in importance within their clans and towns.

The Cherokee found themselves caught between the British and the French, both of whom were invading their mountain home. They played one against the other until the French left North America following the French and Indian Wars in 1763. After this the Cherokee were at the mercy of the British. The Cherokee population was devastated by smallpox epidemics in 1738 and 1750—just as settlers were pushing into the mountains. Warriors tried to keep the settlers away, but there was a never-ending wave of them. "You will find the settlement of this land dark and bloody," Dragging Canoe, a great chief, said at the time. Several Cherokee towns joined the British in fighting the settlers during the Revolutionary War. When the American colonies won their independence, the Cherokee found it more difficult to defend their ancestral home. "Whole nations have melted away like balls of snow before the sun," said Dragging Canoe in an address to the Cherokee council in 1775.

The Cherokee signed several treaties with the United States in which they agreed to give up some parts of their homeland, if they were allowed to keep others. Yet their conflict with the newcomers became as much a cultural struggle as a war for land. How could they match the technology of rifles and gunpowder? The settlers also had metals—iron, silver, and lead—along with the knowledge and skill to fashion useful tools. They farmed the land efficiently and made good, warm clothing as well as other household articles. White people also had a written language and mathematics, and they had their own music—the Cherokee were amazed that such a beautiful sound could issue from an odd-shaped box like the fiddle.

The Cherokee adopted the farming practices of the settlers. They built cabins, cleared fields, and traded for tools, such as this ox yoke.

*W*alking behind his ox, this Cherokee man is plowing in the same manner as the farmers of European descent who settled in the mountains.

The Cherokee wanted European goods and knowledge. In exchange, they sold beaver pelts. When these became scarce, they sold Creek captives as slaves, and then they sold their land. As Christian missionaries converted people and white traders married native women, the Cherokee began to adopt European ways of life, including clothing, household goods, and housing. Like some settlers, they farmed the land, and a few even owned African-American slaves. George Washington furnished the Cherokee with spinning wheels and cotton seeds, and women made clothes from the cotton they grew in their fields. Shamans argued against these European influences because they feared that the Cherokee would lose their identity as a people.

Cherokee Language

In 1809, a mixed-blood Cherokee named Sequoyah, also known as George Gist and George Guess, began a twelve-year project in which he invented a Cherokee syllabary, a kind of alphabet, so the tribe would have a written language. The alphabet, which Sequoyah called "talking leaves," consisted of eighty-five characters representing each of the different sounds in the Cherokee language. Sequoyah was the only person in history to create an alphabet entirely on his own. With the written language, the Cherokee were able to operate a printing press with which they published their own constitution and a newspaper called the *Cherokee Phoenix*.

The Cherokee language is quite fascinating, but it can also be challenging for non-native speakers. It does not have several consonants found in English and contains a few sounds not commonly found in Western languages. There are also several dialects—two in Tennessee and the Carolinas, and a separate Oklahoma Cherokee that is a blend of several dialects spoken by those who migrated west. The Cherokee language relies heavily on subtle changes of pitch or tone, which are sometimes difficult to translate to the Roman alphabet. To help you pronounce Cherokee words, here is a list of vowels and consonants, along with their sounds. The examples are based on the *Cherokee-English Dictionary* published by the Cherokee Nation of Oklahoma.

a   as in father
e   as in echo

i	as in sit
o	as in hello
u	as in rule
v	as in cut

The letter "v" represents a vowel that is similar to the "u" in "cut," but with a deeper nasal sound. Cherokee vowels may be long or short. Most often, vowels at the end of a syllable are relatively long. Vowels in the middle of syllables are short.

Consonants are generally pronounced as in English, except that "g" is always hard, as in "go." There are no sounds in the Cherokee language for the consonants "b," "p," or "z." The question mark (?) is used for a sound known as the glottal stop that is common to many Indian languages. Like a short breath or catch in the throat, it is similar to the sound between the first and second "oh" in "oh-oh," or the sound in place of the "t" in the Cockney pronunciation of "bottle."

Here are some examples of everyday words that you might say in Cherokee.

acorn	gule
boy	achuja
brother	udo
cat	wesa
child	ayohli
corn	selu
crow	koga
deer	ahawi

dog	gihli
earth	elohi
father	edoda
fish	aja?di
forest	inage?i
friend	unali?i
frog	walosi
girl	agehyuja
hello	osiyo, siyo (two different versions)
home	juwenvsv?i
house	gahljode
moon	nvda
mother	uji
mountain	odalv?i
no	hla
rabbit	jisdu
river	uweyv?i
sister	udo
squirrel	saloli
sun	nvdo
thank you	wado
valley	ukedaliyv?i
water	ama
yes	vv

Cherokee Alphabet

D *a*	R *e*	T *i*	Ꮺ *o*	Ꮕ *u*	i *v*
S *ga* Ꭴ *ka*	Ᏺ *ge*	Ᏺ *gi*	A *go*	J *gu*	E *gv*
Ꮣ *ha*	Ᏸ *he*	Ꭿ *hi*	Ꮖ *ho*	Ᏻ *hu*	Ꮗ *hv*
W *la*	Ꮄ *le*	Ꮅ *li*	Ꮣ *lo*	M *lu*	Ꮑ *lv*
Ꮬ *ma*	Ꮉ *me*	H *mi*	Ꮵ *mo*	Ᏸ *mu*	
Ꮎ *na* Ꮏ *hna* Ꮐ *nah*	Ꮑ *ne*	Ꮒ *ni*	Z *no*	Ꮓ *nu*	Ꮕ *nv*
Ꮖ *qua*	Ꮗ *que*	Ꮙ *qui*	Ꮖ *quo*	Ꮜ *quu*	Ꮛ *quv*
Ꭴ *sa* Ꮝ *s*	Ꮞ *se*	Ꮟ *si*	Ꮠ *so*	Ꮡ *su*	Ꮢ *sv*
� *da* W *ta*	Ꮥ *de* Ꮦ *te*	Ꮧ *di* Ꮨ *ti*	Ꮩ *do*	S *du*	Ꮫ *dv*
Ꮬ *dla* Ꮭ *tla*	L *tle*	Ꮯ *tli*	Ꮰ *tlo*	Ꮱ *tlu*	Ꮲ *tlv*
Ꮳ *tsa*	Ꮴ *tse*	Ꮵ *tsi*	K *tso*	J *tsu*	Ꮷ *tsv*
Ꮹ *wa*	Ꮺ *we*	Ꮻ *wi*	Ꮼ *wo*	Ꮽ *wu*	6 *wv*
Ꮿ *ya*	B *ye*	Ꮥ *yi*	Ꮙ *yo*	G *yu*	B *yv*

Sounds represented by vowels.

a as *a* in *father* or short as *a* in *rival*
e as *a* in *hate* or short as *e* in *met*
i as *i* in *pique* or short as *i* in *pit*
o as *aw* in *law* or short as *o* in *not*
u as *oo* in *fool* or short as *u* in *pull*
v as *u* in *but*, nasalized.

Consonant Sounds.

g nearly as in English, but approaching to k.. d nearly as in English, but approaching to t.. h, k, l, m, n, q, s, t, w, y, as in English. Syllables beginning with g, except Ꮝ have sometimes the power of k, a, s, ɯ, are sometimes sounded to, tu, tv; and syllables written with tl, except Ꮮ sometimes vary to dl.

Pendleton's Lithography, Boston.

With their own alphabet, the Cherokee had the ability to communicate among themselves with the power of a written language.

The words for sun and moon are the same. They are distinguished by adding a second word to mean "dwelling in the day" or "dwelling in the night."

Cherokee Moons

January	Month of the Cold Moon	du no lv ta ni
February	Month of the Bony Moon	ka ga li
March	Month of the Windy Moon	a nu yi
April	Month of the Flower Moon	ka wa ni
May	Month of the Planting Moon	a na a gv ti
June	Month of the Green Corn Moon	de ha lu yi
July	Month of the Ripe Corn Moon	gu ye quo ni
August	Month of the end of the Fruit Moon	ga lo nii
September	Month of the Nut Moon	du li i s di
October	Month of the Harvest Mon	du ni nv di
November	Month of the Trading Moon	nu da de qua
December	Month of the Snow Moon	v s gi ga

Trail of Tears

During the relatively peaceful time of the early 1800s, palisades gradually disappeared from Cherokee villages. Council houses

The only man in human history to create a syllabary entirely on his own, Sequoyah is understandably held in high esteem by the Cherokee.

*B*y *the early 1800s, most Cherokee people lived in log cabins on small farms.*

were no longer built, and traditional homes were replaced by log cabins. Outbuildings, including corn cribs, smokehouses, root cellars, and small barns were also modeled after those of settlers. Communities became more scattered throughout the mountains, then were replaced altogether by isolated farmsteads. These small farms had large vegetable gardens and cornfields of five to twenty acres. Men began to tend crops and raise horses, pigs, cattle, and other livestock. The Cherokee began to quarrel among themselves about whether to adopt white practices or keep their own culture. They also argued about whether or not to move to Oklahoma, where American officials wished to relocate them. During these years, the town of New Echota, Georgia, became the capital of the Cherokee Nation.

By embracing Christianity and a white lifestyle, the Cherokee hoped to live in peace in the mountains alongside the settlers. The settlers' hunger for Cherokee lands, however, continued unabated. In 1835, President Andrew Jackson proposed a treaty to remove the Cherokee and other tribes living east of the Mississippi River. Jackson had been known as a great Indian fighter, and many Cherokee had fought with him against other tribes. They had been told that they would be able to keep their land if they did so, and so they felt betrayed by the president's treaty. Although denounced by most Cherokee, the treaty was approved by Congress. "We can never forget these lands," said Major Ridge, a Cherokee chief who negotiated the treaty of removal, "but an unbending, iron necessity tells us we must leave them. I would willingly die to preserve them, but any forcible effort to keep them will cost us our lands, our lives, and the lives of our children." Upon signing the Treaty of New Echota, he said, "I have signed my death warrant."

In 1838, 16,000 Cherokee were forced to give up their ancestral lands. Private John G. Burnett, who served as an interpreter in the removal, wrote, "I saw the helpless Cherokee arrested and dragged from their homes, and driven at the bayonet point into the stockades. And in the chill of a drizzling rain on an October morning I saw them loaded like cattle or sheep into six hundred and forty-five wagons and started toward the west."

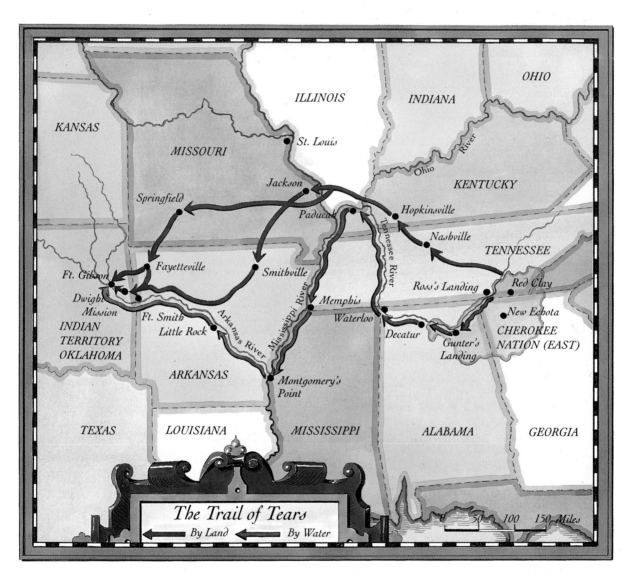

The tragedy of the Trail of Tears will forever be carved into the hearts and minds not only of the Cherokee, but of all people who share their grief and suffering.

Burnett vividly recalled, "On the morning of November the 17th we encountered a terrific sleet and snow storm with freezing temperatures and from that day until we reached the end of the fateful journey on March the 26th, 1839, the sufferings of the Cherokee were awful. The trail of the exiles was a trail of death. They had to sleep in the wagons and on the ground without fire. And I have known as many as twenty-two of them to die in one night of pneumonia due to ill treatment, cold, and exposure."

The Trail of Tears became a seven-hundred-mile journey "with four thousand silent graves reaching from the foothills of the Smoky Mountains to what is known as Indian territory in the West." Women, children, and men died, including the wife of Chief John Ross. Many Native American tribes suffered the loss of their land and forcible relocation, but the Trail of Tears has come to symbolize the displacement of all Indians, just as the tragic Sioux defeat at Wounded Knee represents all massacres.

During this tragic journey, a story was born. According to the legend of the Cherokee Rose, God, looking down from heaven, decided to honor the brave Cherokees. So, as the blood of the warriors and the tears of the women splashed onto the ground, he changed each drop into a beautiful flower—the Cherokee Rose.

This is why today the flowers are so plentiful in Oklahoma, at the end of the Trail of Tears. The state flower of Georgia, once the Cherokee ancestral home, is also the Cherokee Rose.

Endless Trail by Jerome Richard Tiger. Among the worst hardships of this forced march was the extreme cold. Many Cherokee—mostly children, women, and old men—died from exposure.

6. New Ways

The Cherokee who survived the Trail of Tears had to adapt to a new land far from their ancestral home.

THE SURVIVORS OF THE TRAIL OF TEARS HAD TO ESTABLISH THEMSELVES in Indian Territory in what is now the northeast corner of Oklahoma. On reaching their destination, the travelers found some of their people who had gone west ahead of them, including the Arkansas Cherokee as well as members of the party who had agreed to the Treaty of New Echota. These three groups shared the land but did not always get along.

The Cherokee who had opposed removal were the largest group. They formed a national party, which excluded the others. Some members of the party tried to resolve the conflicts among the Cherokee, but those who had opposed the treaty were so angry at the loss of their homeland that they murdered three members of the national party, including Major Ridge. In the aftermath, hostilities deepened, but by 1846, John Ross, Stand Watie, and other leaders were able to unify the Western Cherokee and start to build a new nation.

Western Band

The Western Cherokee established a newspaper called the *Cherokee Advocate*, which published news, editorials, and advertisements in both Cherokee and English. This helped to inspire the dislocated people. The Western Cherokee also set up their own schools, and with a new capital city at Tahlequah, they worked hard to maintain their identity as native people.

Just as the Cherokee were making a new home for themselves, the Civil War was declared. As slaveholders from a southern region, most Cherokee supported the Confederacy. Their territory became a battleground, and by the end of the war they were once again devastated. In 1866, the Western Cherokee were admitted back into the United States when they agreed to free their slaves, allow the Delaware and Shawnee Indians into their Nation, and permit railroad companies to lay tracks across their land.

Over the years, the Western Cherokee further suffered from a lack of good leadership. Their leaders, selected by the United States president, seldom represented the best interests of the Cherokee people. One faction, now known as the Keetoowah Band, protested by retreating into the hills to follow the traditional Cherokee way of life, just as the Eastern Cherokee had struggled against European influences a century before.

In 1889, a commission was formed to abolish the Western Cherokee reservation and open the territory to non-Indian settlement. The land held by the Cherokee was to be divided into plots called allotments. The government sold the surplus land to settlers. Many Cherokee, unfamiliar with business practices, were cheated out of their small allotments. In 1907, the Cherokee were allowed to become United States citizens, but they lost the right to their own government and much of their land.

Mountain Home

Back in the southern Appalachian Mountains, the farms that the Cherokee had left behind were taken over by settlers. The Cherokee had never locked their doors. They had practiced rituals

Many Cherokee keep alive the traditions of their people. Here, a man proudly demonstrates how the water drum was properly used in the square ground.

with tobacco or wood that had been struck by lightning to protect their homes from evil spirits—but this hardly stopped the settlers. Many of the settlers moved right into Cherokee cabins, some of which are still occupied today. Cherokee paths through the mountains and valleys became wagon roads for settlers and eventually the highway systems that now cut across the land.

Not all Cherokee followed the Trail of Tears during the 1838 removal; some had fled into the mountains. There they eluded the soldiers in the thick foliage and shadows. The Cherokee have a spell for making themselves invisible to enemies in which they chant, "The wind will take me away, and no one but I alone will know it. Trees! Trees! Trees! Trees! It will be swaying them, and they will be with me." Or, "I will pretend to be a leaf from a tree: people will see me, but they will carelessly step over me."

Yet, for many years, these people struggled for survival—they could not own land and they were not considered citizens. Over time, with the help of Colonel Will Thomas—a settler who became a good friend of the Cherokee and an adopted member of the tribe—they quietly bought lands that were held in his name. These people were considered outlaws on their own land until 1870, when the federal government at long last recognized their claims. With difficulty, they were able to establish title to the lands that were held in Thomas's name.

Known as the Eastern Cherokee, they now live on a reservation called the Qualla Boundary—the largest Indian reservation in the South—which was formally established in 1889. Many people think "Qualla" is a Cherokee word. Actually, the reservation of the Eastern Band of the Cherokee came to be called Qualla Boundary because an old Indian woman, whose English name was Polly, lived near Thomas's trading post on Shoal Creek. Because there is no "p" sound in their language, the Cherokee called her "Qualla," and the Qualla Post Office came to be established at the trading post. When Will Thomas acquired the land for the Eastern Cherokee, it was called the Qualla Boundary.

The Cherokee Today

Today, the Eastern Band of the Cherokee maintains its own council house and government on the Cherokee Reservation at the edge of the Great Smoky Mountains in western North Carolina. The Cherokee have sovereignty over their land and the members of their tribe; they form their own nation. They hold elections in which tribal leaders campaign for office. At last count, there were nearly nine thousand enrolled members of the Eastern Band, of whom five thousand were living on the reservation.

Much of the traditional culture has been kept alive on the reservation. Most Cherokee speak English, but their language is taught at home and in school, along with Sequoyah's syllabary. Members of clans live near each other in communities scattered throughout the reservation. Native foods, including chestnut bread, bean bread, and bean dumplings are served in Cherokee homes. Following the old customs, the Cherokee sing and tell stories. Young people favor jeans and T-shirts, but old women still

*T*he Cherokee carved many kinds of masks for ancient dances. With mallet, wedge, and carving knife, craftsmen still create the masks from blocks of wood.

wear long skirts and bright kerchiefs. They have their own newspaper, *Cherokee Feather*, which reports high school football games and prizes at the county fair, along with information about traditional arts and crafts.

The Cherokee hold many public ceremonies from April to October, notably "Unto These Hills," a dramatic interpretation of their life. These events help to strengthen their identity as a people and introduce visitors to Cherokee history. With their population growing, the Eastern Cherokee have come to rely on tourism to support themselves. They have a strong tribal government through which they keep the traditions of their ancestors alive.

The Western Cherokee have struggled for survival through the twentieth century. At one time it was thought that American Indians, including the Cherokee, were destined for extinction. During the Great Depression of the 1930s, President Franklin D. Roosevelt introduced many programs as part of the New Deal to help the American people, including the Cherokee. In 1933, he appointed John Collier as commissioner of Indian affairs. Through the Indian Reorganization Act, money was set aside to purchase land for Indians. Although this law did little to help the Western Cherokee directly, John Collier helped to restore the nation's respect for American Indians. Some thirty years later, the Western Cherokee were awarded 15 million dollars in a lawsuit against the federal government, because the United States had forced them to sell their land in 1893. They used this money to purchase land and to build a cultural center.

In 1970, the Western Cherokee regained the right to elect their own leaders. In 1975, they adopted a new constitution, which helped to strengthen the Cherokee Nation of Oklahoma. Today, the Cherokee of Oklahoma are thriving. Many Western Cherokee live near the historic capital at Tahlequah, as well as in the region around Sallisaw, Oklahoma, where Sequoyah made his home.

Today, there are over 300,000 descendants of the Cherokee living throughout the United States. Although they lost most of their ancestral homeland, the spirit of the Cherokee remains very much alive. N. Scott Momaday, an author of Kiowa Cherokee descent, expresses their deep attachment to the earth and its creations, "Once in his life a man ought to concentrate his mind upon the remembered earth, I believe. He ought to give himself up to a particular landscape in his experience, to look at it from as many angles as he can, to wonder about it, to dwell upon it. He ought to imagine that he touches it with his hands at every season and listens to the sounds that are made upon it. He ought to imagine the creatures there and all the faintest motions of the wind. He ought to recollect the glare of noon and all the colors of the dawn and dusk."

More About

the Cherokee

Time Line

1540 Spanish explorer Hernando de Soto travels through Cherokee country

1629 The Cherokee begin to trade with English settlers

1721 Charleston Treaty with the governor of the Carolinas is thought to be first Cherokee concession of land

1759 Cherokee chiefs are imprisoned by English soldiers

1776 The Cherokee side with the British in the Revolutionary War

1785 Treaty of Hopewell is the first agreement between the United States and the Cherokee

1791 Treaty of Holston calls for "civilization" of the Cherokee by providing farm tools and technical advice

1802 Thomas Jefferson signs Georgia Compact supporting Indian removal

1817 Treaty provides for land in Arkansas. A group of Cherokee migrate voluntarily and establish government there, but are soon forced to move into Indian Territory

1821 Sequoyah finishes the Cherokee syllabary which promotes literacy among the Cherokee

1822 Cherokee supreme court is established

1824 First written laws of the Western Cherokee are enacted

1825 New Echota, Georgia, becomes the Cherokee capital

1827 Cherokee Nation is established with the passage of a democratic constitution and election of John Ross as chief

1828 The *Cherokee Phoenix* is published in English and Cherokee

1828–1830 Georgia legislature abolishes tribal government and claims authority over Cherokee lands

1832 U.S. Supreme Court supports tribal sovereignty in *Worcester* v. *Georgia*, but President Andrew Jackson opposes the decision and Georgia holds a lottery for Cherokee lands

1835 Cherokee leaders agree to surrender their homeland to the United States in the Treaty of New Echota

1838–1839 On the Trail of Tears the Cherokee are exiled from their homeland to Indian Territory in present-day Oklahoma

1844 The *Cherokee Advocate* is established as the first newspaper in Indian territory

1846 A seven-year war among the Western Cherokee in Oklahoma comes to an end

1851 Cherokee Male and Female Seminaries established. The Female Seminary is the first school for girls west of the Mississippi River

1859 Original Keetoowah Society is organized in Oklahoma to maintain Cherokee traditions and to fight slavery

1861 Western Cherokees become allies of the Confederacy in the Civil War

1866 Tribal land rights in Oklahoma are limited when the Cherokee are forced to negotiate peace with the United States after the Civil War

1870 United States recognizes the Cherokee people as American citizens

1876 The Eastern Cherokee are awarded 50,000 acres of Qualla Boundary land in present-day North Carolina

1887 General Allotment Act requires individual ownership of lands held in common by Western Cherokee

1889 Qualla Boundary, the largest reservation in the South, is formally established in North Carolina

1905 Land allotment begins after an official census of Western Cherokees is taken

1907 Oklahoma becomes a state and dissolves Cherokee tribal government

1934 Indian Reorganization Act establishes a land base for tribes and a legal means for self-government

1941–1945 Over 1,000 Cherokee serve in the United States military during World War II

1961 Western Cherokees are awarded $15 million in a lawsuit against the United States government

1985 Wilma Mankiller is elected principal chief of the Cherokee Nation in Oklahoma

1988 Cherokee Nation joins Eastern Band in observing the 150th anniversary of the Trail of Tears

1990 Wilma Mankiller signs historic self-government agreement in which the Cherokee Nation in Oklahoma assumes responsibility for federal funds formally administered by the Bureau of Indian Affairs

1994 Wilma Mankiller announces that she will not run for re-election

1995 Joe Byrd and Garland Eagle elected principal chief and deputy chief

Notable Cherokee People

Many distinguished men and women have made great contributions to the history of the Cherokee people. Here are some well-known Cherokees, many of whom speak for themselves.

Attakullakulla (about 1700–1778), meaning "Leaning Wood," was also known as Onacona, or White Owl, and Little Carpenter because of his small stature. In 1730, he journeyed with a delegation to the royal court of London, and in 1738 he became the peace chief of the Cherokee Nation. A gifted orator, he was friendly with the British and worked with the war chief Oconostota to help colonists live peacefully with his people. Despite his pro-British sentiments, Attakullakulla sided with the Americans during the Revolutionary War and helped to raise an army of five hundred Cherokee warriors to fight on their side.

Bloody Fellow (active in late 1700s), also known as Iskagua and Clear Sky, was a leader of the Chickamauga Cherokee of eastern Tennessee. Armed and supplied by the British, he and Dragging Canoe raided American

Elias Boudinot

settlements during and after the Revolutionary War. In 1791, he engaged in peace talks with President George Washington in Philadelphia, then the nation's capital, but continued his raids, playing the Spanish against the Americans. He finally signed the Treaty of Tellicoo Blockhouse in 1794 and ended hostilities toward settlers in the Southeast.

Elias Boudinot (about 1803–1839), also called Galegina, Buck Watie, and Stag Watie, was the first editor of the *Cherokee Phoenix* newspaper. Brother of Stand Watie, nephew of Major Ridge, and cousin of John Ridge, he was among the group that traveled to Washington to speak with President Andrew Jackson about the removal of the Cherokee from their homeland. An early opponent of removal, he eventually joined the Treaty Party. "I have come to the unpleasant and disagreeable conclusion that our lands, or a large portion of them, are about to be seized and taken from us," he said in an address to Congress. Helping to negotiate the Treaty of New Echota, he was assassinated on the same day as his uncle, Major Ridge (see page 109).

Bowl (1756–1839), also known as Colonel Bowles, was named after the bowl *diwali* that holds the "black drink" used in Cherokee rituals. Siding with the British in the American Revolution, he fought with the Chickamauga under Dragging Canoe. In 1794, he led a raid against a settlement on the Tennessee River in present-day Alabama. When the Cherokee council denounced his action, known as the Massacre of Muscle Shoals, he and his followers fled across the Mississippi River and settled in Arkansas, later moving to Texas. Bowl became a lieutenant colonel in the Mexican army, but when Texas won independence from Mexico, he had to negotiate another treaty to keep his people's land. However, the treaty was never ratified by the Texas senate, and troops were sent to remove the Cherokee. When the Cherokee refused to leave, they were attacked. Bowl was killed in this massacre and was found clutching a metal box that held the 1836 treaty.

Bushyhead, Dennis Wolf (Unaduti) (1826–1898) was the son of a Presbyterian minister. He attended mission schools in the East and in 1841 was a member of a Cherokee delegation to Washington. In 1844, he entered Princeton University but had to return to Oklahoma to take over his deceased father's business interests. In 1848, he became clerk of the Cherokee National Committee, but the next year he headed for California, where he hoped to make a fortune in the gold rush. He stayed for twenty years before settling in Tahlequah. In 1871, he became treasurer of the Cherokee Nation in Oklahoma, and in 1879 he was made principal chief. During his two terms as chief (1879–1887), he urged compromise between the traditionalist full-bloods, notably the militant Keetoowah Society, and the mixed-bloods, who favored assimilation. He encouraged the education of his people and economic development through the leasing of land for railroads, logging, mining, and cattle grazing. A staunch supporter of the General Allotment Act, he died in 1898, just a few years before Oklahoma became a state.

Jess Chisholm (about 1805–1868), the son of a Scottish trader and a Cherokee mother, was born in Tennessee. Around 1816, his family moved to a Cherokee community in western Arkansas. He became a fur trader, but because of his knowledge of the region and fluency in fourteen Indian languages, he also worked as a valued guide and interpreter for military expeditions. Chisholm ran three trading posts in Indian Territory—at Oklahoma City, Lexington, and Camp Holmes. During the Civil War, he negotiated treaties between Indian tribes and the Confederacy but then moved with Opothleyaholo's band near Wichita, Kansas, to maintain his neutrality. There he married the daughter of fellow trader James Edwards and had thirteen children with her. At the end of the war in 1865, he took a wagonload of goods through Indian Territory to the Red River country of Texas to trade with local tribes. He returned with buffalo hides, his wagon cutting ruts in the prairie, thereby blazing the famous Chisholm Trail. Through the 1880s, longhorn cattle were driven along the eight-hundred-mile trail from San Antonio, Texas, to Abilene, Kansas.

Jack Dempsey

Jack Dempsey (1895–1983), the heavyweight boxing champion of the world from 1919 to 1926, once said his mother "had a strain of Cherokee Indian on her mother's side, which enabled her to see and hear things the rest of us couldn't. At least that's what we thought when we were children. Later we realized she was just smart."

Dragging Canoe (Tsiyu-Gunsini) (about 1730–1792), the son of the peace chief Attakullakulla and a cousin of Nancy Ward, was born at Running Water Village, or Natchez Town, along the Tennessee River. As a leader, he violently opposed white settlement, refusing to sign the Treaty of

Sycamore Shoals in 1775, which ceded much of the land that is now Kentucky and northern Tennessee. Accepting arms from the British, he attacked Appalachian settlements. In 1777, Cherokee leaders relinquished vast stretches of Cherokee land, but Dragging Canoe continued to attack settlers for the next five years. Frontier militias responded by attacking the Chickamauga Cherokee until all their villages were destroyed. In 1782, Dragging Canoe led his followers downriver to present-day Chickamauga, Tennessee, and established the Chickamauga Lower Towns, including his new home Mialaquo. When these towns were destroyed, Dragging Canoe finally sought peace. In 1785, the Treaty of Hopewell established formal borders for Cherokee land, but the American government refused to enforce the treaty. Dragging Canoe responded by attacking squatters, but the Cherokee were forced to cede more land. To the moment of his death in 1791, Dragging Canoe resisted the invasion of his homeland.

Stephen Foreman (1807–1881) was born in Rome, Georgia, one of twelve children of a Scottish trader and a Cherokee mother. After his father died, Foreman moved with his family to Cleveland, Tennessee, where he was educated at a missionary school. He went on to study at the College of Richmond and the Princeton Theological Seminary.

A missionary and educator, Foreman worked on a translation of the Bible into the Cherokee language. He was also an associate editor of the *Cherokee Phoenix* and the *Cherokee Advocate*. Because of his opposition to removal he was briefly imprisoned in 1838, then forced to march on the Trail of Tears. Settling in Indian Territory, Foreman continued to serve as a leader, helping to organize a public school system and becoming its first superintendent. In 1844, he was elected to the supreme court of the Cherokee Nation, and he served as executive councilor from 1847 to 1855. During the Civil War he remained neutral, preferring to work as a missionary in Texas. He returned to Indian Territory after the war and started a church in the former home of Elias Boudinot.

John Jolly (active in early 1800s) was also known as Oolooteskee, Oolooteka, and Ahuludegi. He grew up on Hiwassee Island at the junction of the Tennessee and Hiwassee Rivers. About 1806, he met Sam Houston, who during his childhood spent several years in Tennessee. John Jolly adopted Houston as his son and as a member of the Cherokee tribe. Houston later married one of Jolly's nieces.

In 1818, Houston advised Jolly and his tribe of three hundred people to move west. Traveling by keelboat and flatboat, this group of Cherokee rejoined the Arkansas band headed by Jolly's brother Tahlonteskee. When his brother died, Jolly became principal chief of the Western Cherokee.

Junaluska (about 1795–1858), siding with the United States in the Creek War of 1813–1814, led a group of Cherokee warriors against the Red Stick Creeks. In 1814, at the Battle of Horseshoe Bend, he is believed to have killed a Creek warrior who was about to tomahawk General Andrew Jackson. Junaluska and his warriors swam across the Tallapoosa River and charged the Creek forces in the rear. Through this bold move he was able to save the Americans. He reputedly acquired his name, which means "He Who Tries Repeatedly But Fails," because he swore he would annihilate the Creek Indians during this war. He went on the Trail of Tears, but eventually returned to North Carolina. As a reward for his service to the United States, he was given a large tract of land.

William Keeler

William Keeler (1908–1987), president of Phillips Petroleum Company and principal chief of the Cherokee Nation, once said, "Forgive the past and remove resentment from your hearts. Even the strongest person cannot carry such a burden for long."

George Lowry (active in 1820s–1830s), whose Cherokee name Agili means "He Is Rising," was one of the leaders who agreed to surrender one-third of the remaining Eastern Cherokee lands in 1817. In exchange, the Cherokee people were to receive a tract of land of equal size between the Arkansas and White Rivers. In this treaty, relocation to the West was also to be voluntary. After the forced removal on the Trail of Tears, Lowry became chief of council of the emigrants who formed the new government of the Western Cherokee.

John Lowry (active in early 1800s) led four hundred Cherokee warriors in support of General Andrew Jackson against the Red Stick Creeks in 1813–14. As an ally of the United States, Lowry helped to take the village of Hillabee, Alabama. He also fought in the Battle of Horseshoe Bend, his warriors swimming the Tallapoosa River and attacking the Creeks from the rear.

Wilma Mankiller (1945–) was born in the Indian Hospital at Tahlequah, Oklahoma, and spent her early childhood in Rocky Mountain, Oklahoma. At age eleven, her family moved to California in a relocation program sponsored by the Bureau of Indian Affairs. However, her father was able to get only low-paying jobs that barely supported the large family of eleven children, and Mankiller experienced urban poverty firsthand.

During the 1960s and 1970s, Mankiller was active in community programs in San Francisco. After earning her master's degree, she returned to Oklahoma in 1979, and four years later, she was elected the first woman deputy chief of the Cherokee Nation. In 1985, she was the first woman to be elected chief of the Western Cherokee. She assumed the position when her predecessor resigned, and she was later re-elected. When Indians occupied the island of Alcatraz near San Francisco, she stated that the event "nurtured a sense among us that anything was possible—even, perhaps, justice for native people."

Wilma Mankiller

Moytoy (active in 1720s–1730s) became chief of Tellico village in eastern Tennessee in the early 1700s. To gain the support of the Cherokee people in all seven villages against the French, Sir Alexander Cumming declared Moytoy to be "emperor" of the Cherokee Nation in 1730. Cumming assumed that the chief would side with the British in their efforts against the French. However, Moytoy remained independent and over the next few years even attacked British settlements in the mountains.

Oconostota (about 1710–1785), whose name means "Groundhog Sausage," was a member of the Cherokee delegation that met King George II in England in 1730. War chief of the Cherokee during the 1750s, he fought against the settlers who were pushing into the mountains. In 1760, he started the Cherokee War when he led a Cherokee war party against Fort Prince George, South Carolina. It required two armies to defeat Oconostota, and afterward he and his warriors continued to fight from hideouts in the mountains. In 1763, after many villages were destroyed, he finally signed a peace treaty that ceded large portions of Cherokee lands. During the Revolutionary War, Oconostota sided with his old enemies, the British, against the Americans. Once again, the Cherokee saw their villages attacked and destroyed. Oconostota died in 1783 shortly after turning the leadership of his band over to his son Tuksi.

John Ridge (1803–1839) was the son of Major Ridge and cousin of Elias Boudinot and Stand Watie. He was also known as Ganun'dalegi, which means "One Who Follows the Ridge." Born in Rome, Georgia, he attended the Cornwall Foreign Mission School in Connecticut, where he met his future wife, Sarah Bird Northrup. Returning to Georgia with his bride, Ridge became an important tribal leader. He wrote articles for the *Cherokee Phoenix* and served as interpreter and secretary for several tribal delegations to Washington, D.C. A member of the Treaty Party, which considered removal to be inevitable, he signed the Treaty of New Echota in 1835. Ridge wrote to Andrew Jackson in 1836 to protest the cruel treatment of the Cherokee people by the citizens of Georgia. After he was forced to march on

John Ridge

the Trail of Tears, Ridge was murdered with his father and Elias Boudinot by people who resented their signing of the removal treaty.

Major Ridge (1771–1839) who was also known as Nunna Hidihi, meaning "Man of the Mountaintop," was elected to the Cherokee Council when he was just twenty-one. He eventually became speaker because of his skill as an orator. He received the name "Major" during the Creek War in which he served with General Andrew Jackson. He was one of the leaders of the Treaty Party who negotiated the agreement that relinquished Cherokee homelands. Although he was considered a

Major Ridge

traitor by many of his own people, he felt that he had no choice and that his actions saved many lives. After relocation in Indian Territory, he was killed by opponents of the Treaty of New Echota in 1839.

Will Rogers (1879–1935), the popular "cowboy philosopher" and humorist on radio, screen, and the stage, also wrote his own newspaper column. He often referred to Native Americans in his comments, once saying, "My ancestors did not come over on the Mayflower—they met the boat."

Edward Rose (died 1832 or 1833) was the son of a white trader; his mother was of Cherokee and African heritage. As a young man, he was a pirate on the lower Mississippi River near New Orleans. In 1807, he joined a fur-trading expedition headed by Manuel Lisa but got into a dispute and was fired. Rose settled among the Crow Indians in Montana and Wyoming and learned their language. In the early 1820s he

Will Rogers

John Ross

lived among the Arikaras of North Dakota and became fluent in their language as well. For many years he served as a guide and interpreter on expeditions through the Black Hills, Yellowstone, and other western lands. He rejoined the Crows and became a great war chief. They called him Nez Coupe, or Cut Nose, because of his scarred nose, and Five Scalps because he once single-handedly killed five Blackfeet.

John Ross (1790–1866) was born along the Coosa River in Georgia of a Scottish father and a mother who was part Cherokee and part Scottish. Although raised among the Cherokee, Ross was schooled at home by tutors of European ancestry and attended the academy at Kingston, Tennessee. Like many other Cherokee, he participated in the Creek War as an ally of General Andrew Jackson. When he was twenty-three, he married Quatie, a nearly full-blooded Cherokee.

In 1814, he established Ross's Landing, a trading post and ferry on the Tennessee River at the site of present-day Chattanooga. Active in Cherokee affairs, Ross participated in a Cherokee delegation to Washington, D.C., in 1816. Two years later, he returned to Washington and negotiated the Cherokee Treaty. He also drafted the response to federal demands that the Cherokee exchange their lands for tracts west of the Mississippi River.

In the 1820s, after the Cherokee had established a republican form of government modeled after the United States, Ross advocated education and Christianity in hopes that the Cherokee would be able to govern themselves independently in their own state. He helped to establish New Echota, Georgia, as the national capital and moved his family there. The Cherokee adopted a constitution, as well as a senate and house of representatives, and Ross was elected principal chief in 1828.

Between 1828 and 1831, the state of Georgia stripped the Cherokee of many of their rights, and from 1830 to 1838, Ross led many delegations to Washington to argue on behalf of his people. Yet like so many other Cherokee, Ross was forced to leave his home and march on the Trail of Tears. His wife, Quatie, died on the arduous journey. Upon their arrival in Indian Territory, Ross, Sequoyah, and other peacemakers sought to reunite the Cherokee people. Ross helped write the new constitution and was elected principal chief in 1839. During the Civil War, he sought neutrality, but the Cherokee became even more divided over the question of slavery. For the rest of his life, Ross worked as a leader of his faction of the Cherokee people.

Sequoyah (about 1770–1843), also known as George Gist, devised a unique alphabet for the Cherokee. His name is derived from the Cherokee word *sikwaji* or *sogwili*, meaning "sparrow" or "principal bird." Growing up with his mother near Willstown, Alabama, as a boy Sequoyah tended dairy cattle and made cheese. He broke horses, raised corn, and became a good trader. A hunter and trapper, he was crippled in an accident. Forced to give up his active life, he became an accomplished silversmith.

He married Sarah (Sally) in 1815, after serving with Andrew Jackson in the Creek War. Three years later, he moved his family to Arkansas with Chief Jolly's band. He had already begun his syllabary in 1809 and finally completed the monumental project in 1821. Based on eighty-five characters, the method of writing was formally adopted by the Cherokee National Council, and the syllabary became widely used in publications, including the weekly newspaper, the *Cherokee Phoenix*.

Sequoyah moved with his wife and children to Indian Territory in 1829, where he worked to unite the factions among the Cherokee people. He was the first member of any Indian tribe to be granted a pension. He died while searching for a lost tribe of Cherokee reported to be living in Mexico. About his syllabary, which he called "talking leaves," he said, "I thought that if I could make certain things fast on paper, it would be like catching a wild animal and taming it."

Nimrod Jarrett Smith (about 1838–1893) was born near present-day Murphy, North Carolina. During the Civil War, he served as a sergeant in the Confederate army in an Eastern Cherokee company under the command of Colonel W. H. Thomas, a Cherokee trader. Married to Mary

Tahchee

Guthrie, a woman of European descent, he became the first elected principal chief of the Eastern Cherokee in the 1870s and held the position until his death in 1893. Under his leadership, the Eastern Cherokee regained title to their lands in North Carolina. Smith also created a modern educational system for his people.

Redbird Smith (1850–1918) was born near Fort Smith, Arkansas. As Smith grew up, his family supported the Keetoowah Society, which worked to preserve Cherokee heritage and to protect Cherokees against land grabbers. After the Civil War, the Keetoowah Society became less important because there were no major land disputes threatening the Indians. However, the General Allotment Act of 1887 called for the elimination of tribal land held in common, with 160-acre parcels given to individual members. A principal chief and Cherokee traditionalist, Smith revived the Keetoowah Society and fought against allotment and Oklahoma statehood. He feared that speculators would cheat individuals out of their land and the Cherokee would lose their identity as a people. He lobbied Congress and encouraged Cherokee people not to enroll in the census of 1900. In 1902, Smith was arrested and forced to enroll in the census and accept allotment. In 1905, under protest, the Cherokee became the last people in Indian Territory to agree to allotment. Two years later, Oklahoma became a state, and many of Smith's followers moved to the Cookson Hills in northeastern Oklahoma to preserve their traditional way of life. In 1908, Smith was elected principal chief of the Cherokee. In 1912, he joined with Creek, Choctaw, and Chickasaw leaders to form the Four Mothers Society, leading the political and legal battle to restore tribal and cultural heritage.

Tahchee (about 1790–1850) was born in Turkey Town on the Coosa River in present-day Alabama. He later moved with his family to Arkansas, where Bowl had settled with his band of Cherokee. Raised to be a plains hunter and warrior, as a young man, Tahchee participated in raids on the Osage. Enraged at the 1828 treaty between the Cherokee and the United States, Tahchee crossed the Red River into Texas and attacked the Osage and the Comanche. Declared an outlaw by the U.S. Army, with a five-hundred-dollar reward on his head, Tahchee became a famous renegade on the Great Plains.

For years he raided trading posts and Indian camps, then made his peace with the United States and became an army scout working against the Comanches. He also hunted to provide game for the army. In his later years, he settled down as a farmer along the Canadian River near Fort Gibson.

Tsali (died 1838) lived as a farmer and hunter with his family in Valley Town in the Great Smokies of North Carolina. In the spring of 1838, soldiers came to arrest Tsali and his family and take them to the stockade to await their departure on the Trail of Tears. On the way, his wife stumbled and the soldiers goaded her with their bayonets, which angered Tsali. Speaking in Cherokee, he told his sons and brothers-in-law to be ready when he feigned an injury. Shortly afterward, he pretended to hurt his ankle, and when one of the soldiers approached him, he attacked him. One of his sons, Ridges, and his brother-in-law Lowney jumped the other soldier. The first soldier was killed by his own gun and the other fled into the woods.

That summer Tsali and his family hid out in a cave on Clingman's Dome, a high peak in the Great Smokies. They were joined by three hundred other Cherokee who opposed removal. In the fall, General Winfield Scott sent word through Will Thomas, an adopted Cherokee, that if those responsible for the death of the soldier surrendered, his troops would cease their search for the other fugitives. Tsali, Lowney, and Ridges gave themselves up and, following a military trial, were executed by firing squad. Tsali is now honored as a hero among the Eastern Cherokee.

James Wafford (1806–1896) was born near present-day Clarkesville, Georgia, the grandson of a colonel in the Revolutionary War. His grandfather established Wafford Settlement in 1785 on Cherokee lands, and about a hundred acres were ceded by the tribe in 1804. A cousin of Sequoyah, Wafford's mother was of Cherokee, Natchez, and European ancestry. Also known as Tsuskwanunnawata, meaning "Worn-out Blanket," Wafford attended a mission school at Valleytown, where he worked on a translation of a Sunday school speller. In 1824, he worked for the Census Bureau, gaining valuable knowledge about the Cherokee people and their homeland. During the Trail of Tears, he served as a commander of a group of emigrants and later became a member of the Western Cherokee tribal council. In 1891, James Mooney interviewed him at Tahlequah in Indian Territory for his monumental study of the Cherokee.

Nancy Ward (about 1738–1824) was born into the Wolf Clan at Chota, the old Cherokee capital near Fort Loudon, Tennessee. Also known as Tsiistunagiska, or "Wild Rose," because of her rosy complexion, and Nanye-hi, or "One Who Goes About," she was a sister of Attakullakulla and a cousin of Dragging Canoe. While still a teenager she married Kingfisher, a Cherokee of the Deer clan, and had two children with him.

At the Battle of Taliwa against the Creeks, she helped her husband, and when he died in battle, she took up his musket. For her bravery, she was given the name *ghighau*—beloved woman. She subsequently became head of the Women's Council and voted on the Chief's Council. One of her rights was to pardon condemned captives, and she often spared white captives. She became known as an advocate of peace, and during the American Revolution she warned settlers of impending Cherokee attacks. At the end of the war she advocated reconciliation and friendship. Although many people on both sides of the conflict disagreed with her, there were few who did not respect her.

During this time, she married her second husband, an Irish trader, and had three children with him. She opened a thriving inn at Womankiller Ford on the Ocowee River and became known as "Nancy," a version of her Cherokee name, Nanye-hi. As more people of European descent poured into Tennessee, she became disillusioned with her policy of friendship toward settlers and advised the Cherokee Council of 1817 to cede no more lands and to resist removal—a policy she urged until her death in 1824. Among the Cherokee people, she is still honored for her courage, beauty, and wisdom.

Stand Watie

Stand Watie (1806–1871) was born in Coosawalee near present-day Rome, Georgia. A member of the Deer clan, he was also known as Degataga, meaning "Standing Together as One," "Stand Firm," or "Immovable." Like his older brother, Elias Boudinot, Watie attended school at Brainerd Mission in eastern Tennessee, then worked with his brother on the *Cherokee Phoenix*. Viewing removal as inevitable, he took an active role in the Treaty Party in opposition to John Ross. Along with his uncle and cousin, Major and John Ridge, Watie signed the Treaty of New Echota in 1835. After the Trail of Tears, he was to be killed along with the Ridges and his brother Elias. However, he was warned, and of the four men he was the only one who managed to escape the murderers. He retaliated by setting fire to the home of John Ross.

Helping to reorganize the Cherokee in Indian Territory, Watie was a member of the council from 1845 to 1861, serving as speaker from 1857 to 1859. During the Civil War, he became a Confederate general, leading two Cherokee Mounted Rifles regiments in more battles west of the Mississippi River than any other fighting unit. In 1864, he was elected principal chief of the southern band of Cherokees and was the last Confederate to put down his arms at the end of the Civil War.

In 1866, he helped to negotiate the Cherokee Reconstruction Treaty, then settled down to farm on the Grand River near Bernice in Indian Territory. He married Sarah Caroline "Betsy" Bell, with whom he had five children. Because of his thorough knowledge of Cherokee culture, he became a source for Henry Rowe Schoolcraft's famous study of Native American life.

White Path (1763–1835) was most likely born near Turniptown near present-day Ellijay, Georgia. During the Revolutionary War, under the command of Dragging Canoe, he raided American settlements. However, in the Creek War, he sided with the Americans against William Weatherford and the Red Stick Creeks.

Living on a small farm near Turniptown, White Path also served on the Cherokee National Council. However, he opposed assimilation, and when he spoke out against the new tribal laws and the work of missionaries among the Cherokee, he was ejected from his council seat in disgrace. In 1827, White Path and other traditionalists created another council that opposed the Cherokee constitution drafted under the leadership of John Ross. However, within a few months, White Path's Rebellion lost momentum, and nontraditional accommodations were added into the constitution.

Although he remained an independent spirit, White Path was re-elected to the Cherokee National Council on August 28, 1827.

Yonagusta (about 1760–1839), whose name means "Drowning Bear," was a peace chief of the North Carolina Cherokees, widely known for his diplomacy and oratory. His band lived along the Tuckaseigee River, but in 1819 moved near the Oconoluftee River. When he was about sixty years old, Yonagusta became so ill that he lapsed into a coma. Believing he was dead, his people began to mourn him, but after a day or so, he revived. Claiming he had visited the spirit world, he became a prophet, denouncing the use of alcohol.

In 1829, Yonagusta and fifty-eight other people left the Cherokee Nation and became citizens of Haywood County, North Carolina. Purchasing a tract of land through Yonagusta's adopted son Will Thomas, who had become an attorney, they managed to avoid removal to Indian Territory.

Glossary

Ada 'wehi High priest who headed Cherokee councils

Aniyvwiya Cherokee name for themselves, meaning "real people" or "principal people"

Appalachia Mountainous region of the eastern United States, largely in the Upland South

atayohi Cherokee round dance

breechcloth A cloth or skin worn between the legs; also called breechclout

buckskin Deer hide softened by a tanning or curing process

Cherokee Nation Cherokee people united by common heritage and government

clan A group of families related to a common ancestor

dance ground An open area in which the Cherokee held dances and other important ceremonies; also called square ground

diyelidohi Person who kept order at dances

galûñ lati Cherokee word for the sky

Great Smoky Mountains A mountain range of the southern Appalachians

handbreadth Unit of measure from 2 1/2 to 4 inches

ikkûñyialehûñski Lead singer at dances

Iroquoian A language family of eastern North America, including Cherokee and the Iroquois languages of New York and southern Canada

Kanati Cherokee name for the Great Spirit

lacrosse Modern sport based on a popular woodland Indian ball game

New Echota Town in Georgia that became the latter-day capital of the Cherokee Nation

palisade A strong wall of pointed wooden stakes or logs used as a defense

parched corn Corn that is mixed with wood ashes in a pot or pan and dried over a low fire

Red chief Military or war leader of the Cherokee

river cane Cane similar to bamboo that is split into strips used in weaving baskets

shaman Religious leader with healing powers and a knowledge of medicine

square ground An open area in which the Cherokee held dances and other important ceremonies; also called dance ground

tciloki Creek word for the Cherokee meaning "people of a different speech"

tsiska'gili Cherokee for the red crayfish

uka Chief

Upland South Southern Appalachian Mountains

White chief Civil, or peacetime, Cherokee leader also known as the most beloved man

woodlands culture Way of life including beliefs and customs common among people native to the eastern woodlands of North America

yûñwi tsunsdi The little people of Cherokee folklore

Further Information

Readings

Over the years many excellent books have been written about the Cherokee Nation. Among them, the following were consulted in researching and writing this book:

Chiltoskey, Mary Ulmer. *Cherokee Words with Pictures*. Cherokee, NC: Mary Ulmer and G. B. Chiltoskey, 1972.

Ehle, John. *Trail of Tears: The Rise and Fall of the Cherokee Nation*. New York: Doubleday, 1988.

Feeling, Durbin. *Cherokee-English Dictionary*. Tahlequah, OK: Cherokee Nation of Oklahoma, 1975.

Finger, John R. *Cherokee Americans: The Eastern Band in the Twentieth Century*. Lincoln, NE: University of Nebraska Press, 1991.

Hirschfelder, Arlene, and Kreipe de Montaña, Martha. *The Native American Almanac: A Portrait of Native America Today*. New York: Prentice-Hall, 1993.

Holmes, Ruth Bradley, and Smith, Betty Sharp. *Beginning Cherokee*. Norman: University of Oklahoma Press, 1976.

Hudson, Charles. *The Southeastern Indians*. Knoxville: University of Tennessee Press, 1976.

Johansen, Bruce E., and Grinde, Donald A. Jr. *The Encyclopedia of Native American Biography: Six Hundred Life Stories of Important People from Powhatan to Wilma Mankiller*. New York: Henry Holt, 1997.

Johnson, Michael G. *The Native Tribes of North America: A Concise Encyclopedia*. New York: Macmillan, 1994.

Kilpatrick, Jack Frederick, and Kilpatrick, Anna Gritts. *Run Toward the Nightland: Magic of the Oklahoma Cherokees*. Dallas: Southern Methodist University Press, 1967.

King, Duane H., ed. *The Cherokee Indian Nation: A Troubled History*. Knoxville: University of Tennessee Press, 1979.

Klein, Barry T., ed. *Reference Encyclopedia of the American Indian*. West Nyack, NY: Todd Publications, 1990.

Langer, Howard J., ed. *American Indian Quotations*. Westport, CT: Greenwood Press, 1996.

Lewis, T.M.N., and Kneberg, Madeline. *Oconoluftee Indian Village: An Interpretation of a Cherokee Community of 1750*. Cherokee, NC: Cherokee Historical Association, 1954.

Mails, Thomas E. *The Cherokee People: The Story of the Cherokees from Earliest Origins to Contemporary Times*. Tulsa, OK: Council Oaks Books, 1992.

Mooney, James. *Myths of the Cherokee*. New York: Dover Publications, 1995.

Shanks, Ralph, and Shanks, Lisa Woo. *The North American Indian Travel Guide*. Petaluma, CA: Costano Books, 1993.

Speck, Frank G., and Broom, Leonard. *Cherokee Dance and Drama*. Norman, OK: University of Oklahoma Press, 1983.

Ulmer, Mary, and Beck, Samuel E., eds. *Cherokee Cooklore: Preparing Cherokee Foods*. Cherokee, NC: Museum of the Cherokee Indian, 1951.

Underwood, Thomas Bryan. *Cherokee Legends and the Trail of Tears*. Cherokee, NC: Cherokee Publications, 1995.

Waldman, Carl. *Encyclopedia of Native American Tribes*. New York: Facts on File Publications, 1988.

————. *Who was who in Native American History: Indians and Non-Indians from Early Contacts Through 1900*. New York: Facts on File, 1990.

Wilson, Charles Reagan, and Ferris, William, eds. *Encyclopedia of Southern Culture*. Chapel Hill, NC: University of North Carolina Press, 1993.

Young people who would like to learn more about the Cherokee may be especially interested in reading the following books, which were also consulted in writing this book:

Brill, Marlene Targ. *The Trail of Tears: The Cherokee Journey from Home*. Brookfield, CT: Millbrook Press, 1995.

Claro, Nicole. *The Cherokee Indians*. New York: Chelsea House, 1992.

Fremon, David K. *The Trail of Tears*. New York: Maxwell Macmillan International, 1994.

Lepthien, Emilie U. *The Cherokee*. Chicago: Children's Press, 1985, 1992.

Lucas, Eileen. *The Cherokees: People of the Southeast*. Brookfield, CT: Millbrook Press, 1993.

Lund, Bill. *The Cherokee Indians*. Mankato, MN: Bridgestone Books, 1997.

McCall, Barbara A. *The Cherokee*. Vero Beach, FL: Rourke Publications, 1989.

Perdue, Theda. *The Cherokee*. New York: Chelsea House, 1989.

Sharpe, J. Ed. *The Cherokees Past and Present: An Authentic Guide to the Cherokee People.* Cherokee, NC: Cherokee Publications, 1970.

Sneve, Virginia Driving Hawk. *The Cherokees.* New York: Holiday House, 1996.

Cherokee Organizations

The Cherokee are in the midst of a social and cultural revival. Among the many organizations listed below are museums where skilled craftspeople make shapely baskets, pottery, beadwork (belts and sashes), finger weavings, and wood carvings of masks and dugouts. The Oconoluftee Village, which features a seven-sided council house and examples of early homes and cabins, offers demonstrations and interpretive tours about traditional Cherokee lifeways. The Museum of the Cherokee Indian displays treasures of Cherokee history, and the Qualla Arts and Crafts Mutual offers the finest contemporary crafts.

In Oklahoma, the Cherokee National Historical Society provides interpretive programs at the wonderful reconstructed village of Tsa-La-Gi and displays contemporary artwork at the Cherokee National Museum.

North Carolina
Cherokee Visitor Center
P. O. Box 460
Cherokee, NC 28719
1-800-438-1601
E-mail: chero@drake.dnet.net

Eastern Band of Cherokee Indians
P. O. Box 455
Cherokee, NC 28719
1-704 497-2952

Museum of the Cherokee
U. S. Highway 441 North
Cherokee, NC 28719
1-704-497-3481

Oconoluftee Indian Village
U. S. Highway 441 North
Cherokee, NC 28719
1-704-479-2315

Qualla Arts and Crafts Mutual, Inc.
P. O. Box 310
Cherokee, NC 28719
1-704-497-3103

Oklahoma
Cherokee Heritage Center (Tsa-La-Gi)
P. O. Box 515
Tahlequah, OK 74464
1-918-456-6007

Cherokee Nation of Oklahoma
P. O. Box 948
Tahlequah, OK 74465
1-918-456-0671

Cherokee National Historical Society
P. O. Box 515
Tahlequah, OK 74464

United Keetoowah Band of Cherokee
2450 S. Muskogee Ave.
Tahlequah, OK 74464

Websites

Over the past several years, American Indians have established a strong presence on the Internet. Following is a list of some of the best websites to visit for more information about the Cherokee and other American Indian peoples.

American Indian Who's Hot
http://www.cris.com/~misterg/award/whoshot.shtml
Cherokee Messenger
http://www.powersource.com/powersource/cherokee/default.html
The Cherokee Nation
http://www.powersource.com/powersource/nation/default.html
The Cherokee Nation (Tahlequah)
http://www.tahlequah.com/cherokee/
The Cherokee National Historical Society
http://www.powersource.com/powersource/heritage/default.html
Cherokee Indian Reservation (Eastern Band)
http://www.cherokee-nc.com
The Cherokees of California, Inc.
http://www.Powersource.com/cocinc/
Cherokee of Georgia Tribal Council, Inc.
http://www.tallahassee.net/~cherokee/
The Eastern Band of the Cherokee Indians
http://www.charweb.org/neighbors/na/cherokee.htm
Eastern Band of the Cherokee Tribe
http://www2.ncsu.edu/ncsu/stud_orgs/native_american/nctribes_
org/echerokee.html
First Nations: Histories
http://www.dickshovel.com/Compacts.html
FirstNations.Com
http://www.firstnations.com/
History of the Cherokee
http://www.phoenix.net/~martikw/default.html
Index of Native American Resources on the Internet
http://hanksville.phast.umass.edu/misc/NAresources.html
Native American Navigator
http://www.ilt.columbia,edu/k12/naha/nanav.html
Native American Sites
http://www.pitt.edu/~lmitten/indians.html
NativeWeb
http://www.nativeweb.org/

Northern Cherokee Nation
http://onlinenow.com/kansascitymo/
Northern_Cherokee_Nation/
Travelers Guide to the Cherokee Nation
http://www.powersource.com/powersource/nation/chtrav.html
Tsalagi (Cherokee) Literature
http://www.indians.org/welker/cherokee.htm
Tsa-la-gi Cultural Center of the Cherokee Nation (Tahlequah, Oklahoma)
http://www.ionet.net/~skili/center.html
United Keetoowah Band WWW
http://www.uark.edu/depts/comminfo/UKB/welcome.html

Index

Page numbers for illustrations are in **boldface**.

Raymond Bial

HAS PUBLISHED OVER THIRTY CRITICALLY ACCLAIMED BOOKS OF PHOTOGRAPHS for children and adults. His photo-essays for children include *Corn Belt Harvest, Amish Home, Frontier Home, Shaker Home, The Underground Railroad, Portrait of a Farm Family, With Needle and Thread: A Book About Quilts, Mist Over the Mountains: Appalachia and Its People, Cajun Home,* and *Where Lincoln Walked.*

He is currently immersed in writing *Lifeways,* a series of books about Native Americans. As with his other work, Bial's deep feeling for his subjects is evident in both the text and illustrations. He travels to tribal cultural centers, photographing homes, artifacts, and surroundings and learning firsthand about the lifeways of each of these peoples.

A full-time library director at a small college in Champaign, Illinois, he lives with his wife and three children in nearby Urbana.